The Clueless Investigator

on a very
grateful Sunday
Love & gratitude always!
Liz Sartori

THE CLUELESS INVESTIGATOR

A Conversion Story

LIZ SARTORI

Wildrose Press

Wildrose Press
Orem, UT
wildrose.enterprises@gmail.com

First published in the United States of America in April 2011.

Printed in the United States of America.
10 9 8 7 6 5 4 3 2 1

ISBN-13: 978-0-615486-06-2
ISBN-10: 0615486061

Cover Art: "Detective Girl" istockphoto.com. Used with permission.
Cover Design: LibrisPro, www.librispro.com
Interior Design & Typesetting: LibrisPro, www.librispro.com

Quotation on page 42 from "O My Father," *Hymns*. No. 292. Corporation of the President of The Church of Jesus Christ of Latter-day Saints, 1985.

Quotation on page 61 from *The Hiding Place*.by Corrie Ten Boom with John and Elizabeth Sherril. p.39. Chosen Books: Nov. 1971, Bantam Books: Oct. 1974.

Acknowledgments

I would like to express my gratitude to Virginia Stanton Woods and the James Stanton family for their unparalleled fellowshipping of a new friend at an important time in my life.

Thanks also go to long-time friends Jon and Linda Christensen and their children, now adults; to the Bev and Dave Glazier family; the Lynn and Perry Carter family; Susan and Gordon Ridd; and to Albert and Susanne Loris who convinced me to write this.

I wish to acknowledge several close friends, Rodney and Kim Jackson, Karen and Lewis Church, Linda and Doug Cook, Mary Taylor, and many others in my ward who have supported, helped, and encouraged me over the years.

I also wish to thank my sister, Lois Goodin, for being there for me in recent times during illness and rehabilitation, and Alva Panciera Lamothe, for her encouragement at all times. Alva is a dear, dear friend and my fourth cousin.

Table Of Contents

1

This Is My Story

This was an evening like many others, when I had been asked to present my conversion story to a group. This time it was a Family Home Evening group from the Brigham Young University ward where my friend Albert was in the bishopric. The four members of the bishopric and their families took turns hosting the FHE group in their homes on Monday nights. On this night I was speaking to a group in the home of Albert and Susanne Loris. The room was full and I was presenting my conversion story to new faces.

All went well and when I concluded my presentation, the young men and women enthusiastically expressed their thanks. Several listeners rather excitedly asked me, "*Have you written this down!??*" I had never really thought of doing that before they suggested it.

"Uh, no," I had to answer.

Their question got me thinking. With their enthusiasm and Susanne's support and faith urging me forward, I finally decided it was time to write my story.

This group of young adults continued to interact with me, taking about 100 names on cards to do the temple work for my kindred dead. I have always needed help with this, especially with my male ancestors. In the temple, men are proxies for deceased men; women are proxies for deceased women. This group was a great boon to me and helped me get much needed work completed.

I am a single woman. I am the only person in my family on this side of the veil who is a member of The Church of Jesus Christ of Latter-day Saints. My situation reminds me of what Randy Pausch said in his book, *The Last Lecture*—it's like being known as the tallest of the Seven Dwarfs, a somewhat ambiguous distinction!

I am grateful for the help of the young people of that BYU ward—their help with my temple work and their encouragement to share my story.

This is my conversion story.

An Introduction

My name is Elizabeth Ann Sartori, known to my family and friends as "Liz." What makes me unique? How I define myself: an educator, a life-time student, a sister, a friend, a mentor to students, a genealogy buff, sports fan, and outdoor-girl. I have been fortunate to realize some of my life's dreams. I've made a good dip into the bucket list. My life may not be unique, but it has certainly been varied!

My mother and father were religious people. Mom read Bible stories to us from the *Old Testament Illustrated Children's Bible* when I was four years old. My sisters were three years older and three years younger than me. I can still see the illustrations in my mind's eye: David facing Goliath, Joseph and his "coat of many colors," and Solomon, the great and wise king.

We had a book about Jesus too, with more pictures. Mom listened to our prayers every night before bed. Dad was seldom there to tuck us in, as he worked in a woolen mill from 3:00 until 11:00 p.m. but he fully encouraged us in a life of faith.

My family was not rich but I didn't know it. I remember there was a year, or maybe two, when we didn't have back-to-school clothes because Dad had been laid off at the mill. But this was a minor challenge for me. I hardly noticed what we didn't have because I found so much joy in what we *did* have—my family, the out-of-doors, the things that came with no price tag attached.

We were a solid family. Mom made Dad's lunches and our school lunches until we went to the high school where there was a cafeteria with warm meals. There were family outings at the "upper farm," with all our aunts, uncles and cousins. There were tables topped with great food and blankets spread on the ground in the old lane between the stone walls of the farm.

Food and fun were a large part of our picnics. The spinster aunts, my dad's two sisters, taught us games like "Dock on the Rock" and "Tag." It seemed there was no end to the adventure and laughter at those family get-togethers.

Much of my early life was carefree. Activity and adventure abounded. I rode my cousin Larry's pony, Scout, and a little blue Columbia bicycle all over the farm. Picking wild blueberries, strawberries, and the grapes that grew on the stone walls were some of my favorite things to do. In the winter, my sisters, cousins, and I went sledding and ice skating. We built snowmen and bonfires on the ice.

Mother was a stay-at-home mom with lots to do. In addition to the usual household chores, in the summer and fall she bottled pears, peaches, grape juice, pickles, applesauce, green beans, relishes, tomato juice, and jellies. When I came home from school in the fall, I would sniff the air trying to identify what she was processing and bottling.

We spent many a Saturday or Sunday visiting my maternal grandparents at Echo Farm. The people from my grandparents' generation were immigrants from Europe before the turn of the last century. They all had started with very little but through hard work had built their fortunes into farms of 160 acres or more.

I loved visiting the farms. There were trees to climb, apples to pick, the vegetable garden and a huge grape arbor to tend. There was also the work-horse to watch and feed, and Grandpa's herd of black angus cattle. Once we watched the Good Humor Ice Cream man feed Jerry, the horse, some chocolate-covered ice cream bars. The horse loved those bars, and obligingly spit out the sticks!

We also sometimes called on Mom's childhood friends. She had grown up with five girls, who remained friends into their adulthood. These women and their spouses were her great friends. Their children became our playmates when the grown-ups visited. I particularly recall with great fondness our visits to the Joseph Koran family.

Growing Up in a Tiny Town

I grew up in Connecticut—in Stafford, Tolland County, Staffordville, and then Stafford Springs after sixth grade. I grew up in a relatively small area, where we went to school, church, swimming and skating, sledding and tobogganing, bike riding and hiking.

Staffordville was and still is a small eastern town: one Catholic church, one Protestant church, no library, no restaurant or drive-in, and only one general store, Phelps and Cunningham.

The school I attended had four classrooms, two grades to a room, and no kindergarten. Although it has since doubled in size, the schoolhouse was tiny when I was there. It looked like a square brick house with lots of windows. The school was only a couple of hundred yards from the beach at mile-long Staffordville Lake.

Until I was five years old, our family owned a yellow house on the town square. Many eastern towns have a town square. We lived right there in the center of town, on a relatively busy street with trucks bringing goods, groceries and produce to the store nearby.

I did not like to feel limited by small spaces or places. I wished to wander and explore. Our little back yard was too confining for me. I couldn't see much of the action of the town from there—or maybe I was just eager to head west, even at that early age! At any rate, I would take off on my tricycle, heading west out of town. A number of times my mother or father had to chase after me, catching up when I was nearly a block or two from the house!

The last time I remember taking off to explore the town, I made it three whole blocks distance from the yard. My poor father came after me. He was at his wit's end. He had to do something to discourage my tricycle travel and to teach me to stay within the safe confines of our yard. He took off his belt. He would never have used it, but at the age of four I wasn't sure—so I pedaled toward home for all I was worth!

We moved not long after that and Mom told me later that my antics were considered in that decision. The store was only thirty yards from our home. My parents figured it was only a matter of time before I was harmed. Even at this young age, I had already begun to overuse my guardian angels.

We moved from the yellow house on the town square into a cabin on the "upper farm" because no other homes in the town were available. We lived in the cabin that sat along a dirt road while I was in first and second grades. My grandfather didn't mind having us live there. He liked that there was someone on his land all the time. He was getting older and still living in his tiny house, which we called the "shack," up at the other end of the lane.

My Sartori grandparents came from Austria and northern Italy, where the farmers had summer pasture for their animals in the mountains, and winter pasture and shelter down closer to home. They continued to use this system for pasturing their animals after immigrating to the United States.

We called my grandfather's summer fields and barns the "upper farm." Just before winter, we brought the cows down to the "lower farm" near town, only three miles distance. Bringing down the cows was a festive occasion, just like in the "old country."

Living on the farm was a grand adventure for me, as a five and six-year-old. But for Mom and Dad there was water to carry from the well, lamp glasses to clean (no electricity), and an icebox instead of a refrigerator. Our fresh produce came from Mom's garden; Dad worked in it too, in the mornings. Mom bottled fruit, vegetables, relishes, and juices on a wood stove!

People must not have worried as much in those days, or I led a charmed life, because I wandered all over that farm by myself. Many days I would walk to the spring, far out of sight of the cabin. I think I had ADHD tendencies, long before that diagnosis was invented. I know I tired my Mom out more than my sisters did. She looked at me at times and sighed, saying, "Just watching you makes me tired!" My guardian angels were doing a very good job.

There were so many beautiful things to see in the countryside. The farm was a burst of color in the spring and summer. There were honeysuckle flowers, daisies, bluettes, buttercups, wild strawberry blossoms, and blueberry bushes, in addition to the blossoms on the trees in the orchard. I can remember my mother making a wreath of colored flower blossoms for my older sister, Anita, to bring to school. She wove it from wild flowers found along the side of the dirt road.

Almost every night from spring to fall, we sat out on the porch at dusk, listening to the whippoorwill's song. I realize this sounds like a page out of a Wilson Rawls book—and it was all ours!

After two years in the cabin, we moved from the upper farm down to the lower farm. We lived in the east side of a duplex, with Uncle Charlie's family on the west side. Charlie was Dad's brother, and was due to inherit the farm from Grandpa. I was seven years old then and very active. I got into a lot of trouble with Uncle Charlie because I was always coming up with "creative" ideas and attempting to carry them out. Some of my ideas were great—like using nets made with cheese cloth and coat hangers to catch baby fish in the brook. Some of my other ideas were not so well received.

I watched many westerns on television. One time after watching a show, I determined that I could make a cowboy campfire in the wood lot. It seemed like a good place to build a fire because there was sand and wood scraps. I sent my cousin Larry and my sister Lois to the house to find matches. The campfire incident did not go over well with the grown-ups. We got busted, and I think Larry got spanked.

Another time, I dammed up a little trickle of water to make a pool. That plan didn't sit well either.

At the Staffordville Elementary School, I had many physical outlets for my energies. My class had only four girls in it, so I spent my free time playing games with the boys—baseball, football, and other sports. But even then, Kathleen, my dear friend in third and fourth grade, and I got into trouble and spent time standing in the corner.

It was probably a relief to everyone when our family moved to Stafford Springs. I was beginning seventh grade and my younger sister

Lois was in fourth. Anita was already at the high school and had been bussing from Staffordville for two years.

Challenges in my Youth

Though much of my existence seemed idyllic at the time, there were some hefty challenges, too. A big challenge of a psychological and emotional, religious and spiritual nature began when I was just seven and a half years old. My self-esteem and my sense of security and confidence took a nose-dive one Sunday morning that would have ramifications for years to come.

My entire family on both sides was Roman Catholic. I had received my first holy communion earlier in the year when I turned seven. Two priests served St. Joseph's Parish, where my family attended. Father Caron and Father Morrisey came all the way from Stafford Springs, five miles away. Father Caron was a gentle, soft-spoken man; Father Morrisey was a yell-and-pound-the-pulpit sort of man. The two priests took turns coming to Staffordville.

On one particular Sunday, I had decided to go to confession and communion. I had fasted since midnight the night before to prepare. It was Father Morrisey's turn to officiate. When I went up to the confessional before the service, I knew who was behind that screen. I'd seen him come in and put on his vestments. I was so intimidated, the form prayer, although very well memorized on my part, just wouldn't quite come forth.

"Bless me father, for I have sinned; it has been __ weeks since my last confession..." would not squeeze through my terror-stricken lips.

"B-b-b-b-bl–," I stuttered.

"Bless," intoned the priest loudly.

"B-b-blesss m-m-m–," I stuttered again.

"Bless me," said the priest as loudly as before.

"B-bless m-me, f-f-f–," I stuttered still.

Father Morrisey leaped out of the confessional booth and facing the congregation, he thundered, "This girl doesn't even know how to give a proper confession!"

He motioned me back to my seat in the congregation beside my father. My older sister sat on his other side. Mom was not there; she was home with the baby.

Dad looked so serious. He did not realize how much I needed to be reassured that I was okay, that I had done nothing wrong. Looking back as an adult, I realize he was dealing with too much himself to think to say something to me. But as a child, I felt I had disappointed him. I was sure I was all washed up with Heavenly Father too, at the ripe old age of seven! I could feel the flames of hell licking my toes, about to consume me. That feeling stayed with me for years.

When we got home from church, Dad sent my older sister and me out to play in our Sunday clothes while he and Mom talked. I don't know what was said, but after that, Mom took us to church. Dad stayed home with the baby, only attending church on Christmas and Easter when the family went together.

From that time on, it seemed an invisible ax hung over my neck. After the incident in the confessional, I was reluctant to go to church, but too scared not to go. This dichotomy existed for quite some time. I had a very strong sense of right and wrong, and wanted to do what was right. However, I acted out quite a bit, too. My strong sense of ethics was probably more due to fear than moral courage.

Health challenges began at an early age, too. Ears, nose, and throat difficulties were a problem for me. I was sick a lot and had earaches, sore throat, colds, and ear infections. I was born with only 30 % of my hearing. I had an operation when I was three years old to correct this. I remember Mom laughing when I told her they placed me on an "ironing board" to do the operation!

Many a night I'd wake up crying into my pillow with an earache. Mom would come to my room with a hot water bottle wrapped in a towel. Dad would bring in a demitasse cup with Italian whiskey, sugar and black coffee in it. Thankfully, I slept through most of the pain.

The earaches were weekly during the cold eastern winters of my elementary years. They diminished a little as time went on until the end of high school. To help prevent the earaches, I had to wear hats from spring until fall, and all my jackets had attached hoods. To this day I hate wearing hats!

I remember a special blanket we called the "Indian Blanket." It had v-shaped designs on a blue background. I think any of us would have been very happy with it, but it must have been decided I'd get more use out of it because I spent more time in bed than my healthier sisters. Also, I think our parents felt bad because they couldn't take away my pain entirely, and so they gave me the special blanket for comfort. When I was wrapped in that blanket, it felt like I was wrapped up in their love.

Nosebleeds were another problem. I got them every day in the summer and sometimes at school when it surely wasn't convenient. Our family doctor didn't do much for them. He said that if I had nosebleeds it must mean I *needed* to have nosebleeds. They calmed down by high school and were rare in my college years.

My mother put a lot of stock in what this doctor advised. She went to several doctors in her late twenties because she had significant female problems. The other doctors said she should "have everything out," but Dr. S. did something that enabled her to bear three children–six, nine, and twelve years after she was married. I don't know what he did but Mother felt it was a miracle.

I've already alluded to the problem of hyperactivity. I also had issues with impulsivity. I was never formally diagnosed–those disorders weren't known when I was a child. However, as an adult, I've researched and read much about these problems.

The special education teachers at the school where I taught said I had to be ADHD, and based upon my personal experience and reading, I tend to agree. Those kind teachers explained that the challenge of ADHD also usually came with high intelligence. This fits with my experience and explains why I spent the last two weeks of fourth grade reading books on my own. I'd finished all the textbooks and schoolwork for the year and my teacher needed a way to occupy my time while she helped the other students.

As a child, I tended to drive everyone crazy with my high energy. I *needed* to be doing something. The difficulties of ADHD were never more clear than when we went to visit our two aunts in the city. In the confines of their apartment in Springfield, Massachusetts, I received many doses of "constructive" criticism. I don't think I endeared myself to many, just a few adventuresome friends.

2

My Family

Like all biographies, my beginnings reach backward through time to include the lives of my parents and their parents. Many of my beliefs and attitudes come from the generations before me. I enjoy participating in genealogy, looking back at these ancestors of mine, exploring their stories, their lives, and coming to know them, not just as my progenitors, but as people, and sometimes, even as friends.

Peter and Suzanna Wargo

My mother, Susan Wargo, was born in Upper Lehigh, Pennsylvania, the oldest of eight children born to Suzanna and Peter Wargo. Suzanna and Peter had immigrated from Slovakia and Hungary and were immediately welcomed into the community of coal miners in Upper Lehigh where everyone spoke Slovak.

The Hungarian surname of Wargo was originally known as Varga, meaning "shoemaker." Like so many other foreign surnames, it was changed at Ellis Island as my grandparents entered the United States. Peter pronounced the "V" like a "W" and someone wrote the "a" at the end hastily, causing it to resemble an "o." Hence the name, Wargo.

The Wargos came to America before the turn of the last century, during a time when there was a great influx of immigrants from Europe. There had been too little food and not enough work. Add to this the threatened conscription into the army for Peter, and the Wargos made the decision to immigrate.

Grandpa Wargo had a marvelous work ethic. It brought him success and land in the new country—something he couldn't have in the "old country" where they were part of the peasant class. Married at 17 years of age, Suzanna and Peter came to American aboard the ship, *Princess Irene*. Peter went to work in the coal mines with his brother, Great Uncle John. Three children were born during this time.

My Mother's Heritage

Susan had many responsibilities growing up. When she was five years old, the family moved from Pennsylvania to Connecticut. Peter bought a small farm in Leonard District, Stafford Hollow. At a time when miners "owed their soul to the company store," he somehow saved enough money to buy the land in Connecticut. No black lung for him!

Grandpa Wargo was very intelligent. He spoke three languages and understood three more. With only one year of formal education, he could add figures fast. When the stores started selling milk from their coolers, he knew to switch from a dairy farm to beef cows. He loved the land; he loved the farm. His sons did not love farming the way he did. They probably would have taken to farming more if he had been less of a taskmaster and more of a father and co-worker.

The boys came of age and joined the military, or were conscripted, at the onset of World War II. Susan and her sister Ethel learned to sew beautifully. They started on Grandma's treadle Singer sewing machine, but as soon as they could, they got their own electric ones.

Grandpa Wargo sold the farm a few years after Grandma died, but in its prime, Echo Farm was 160 acres and included a vineyard, apple orchard, fields and pastures, two big red barns, and a large white farmhouse on the hill facing the barns below. There were out-buildings, a woodshed, a chicken coop, a pig sty, and a separate garage. A long driveway went from the road all the way up and around the house, then back down to the road.

Peter Wargo had mellowed a lot by the time he became a grandfather, when his worries were past and his holdings secure. I spent many, many companionable hours with him working in the wood lot, haying, walking up to the pastures to find woodchucks to trap or to shoot with the 22. Grandpa waged a constant battle with the woodchucks because they ate his garden. We also spent many pleasant afternoons studying his fish pond up in the fields, a distance from the house.

The family spoke Slovak in the home until Susan and Peter Jr. went to school. They studied in a one-room schoolhouse that housed all eight grades. Susan came home from school her first day and exclaimed, "There are adults going to my school!"

Peter and Suzanna learned English when Susan and Peter Jr. brought it home with their school work. At first, this was hard for Susan as her father wanted her to pronounce every letter in every written word like it was pronounced in Slovak and Hungarian. What a relief it was for Susan when her father learned how English is written and pronounced!

Susan helped her mother in the kitchen and with the younger children. She also worked in the garden. The boys helped Peter deliver milk to his customers. They also helped with the bottle washing, haying, and feeding the cows. Sometimes Susan had to help with the haying too, especially if a storm was coming.

Peter thought that girls did not need an education so after the eighth grade, Susan went to work in the Hydeville Woolen Mill. She had to turn her paycheck over to her father until she was 21 years old. At 21, she was able to keep her own money. Right away, she got an eye operation that turned her right eye straight forward instead of pulling toward the side. She also bought her own Chevy Coupe with a rumble seat. It was her pride and joy.

My mother never allowed any name-calling in our home because she knew how it felt to be teased. She had been the brunt of many jokes due to that right eye. We never heard one naughty word in my parents' home either, and that is quite a commendable record!

In Pennsylvania, the Wargo family worshiped as Catholics, in the Greek Catholic Rite. When they moved to Connecticut, they went to the Roman Catholic church and were devout parishioners. The children were brought up strictly, "European style," as Mother called it. Susan's mother said her rosary when her work was done. I remember Grandmother sitting in her favorite rocking chair in the living room. She was a gentle soul. Her kindly ways and soft-spoken words added much by way of good example. I don't remember any preaching. There was no need.

One time my sisters were out in the orchard, picking apples off the ground under the trees to clean up and give the cows a treat. I had an upset stomach that day and spent some time in the bathroom while much of the apple picking was happening. When my sisters were paid some change for their work, Grandma felt bad for me and gave me a little change too. It's easy to remember charity received.

Grandma wore cotton house-dresses with matching aprons every day, except on Sunday when she wore her "Sunday dress" to church. She changed back as soon as she got home. She had serviceable black shoes, and often wore felt slippers in the house. She looked as kindly as she was, with her hair pinned up on top of her head.

Grandma made foods that were common to the Baltic countries: lots of noodles and cabbage dishes with deep-fried vegetables. Mom cooked many of the same foods, as well as the "American" dishes. I was in college before I learned that most people ate their cauliflower steamed gray, instead of the golden-brown, deep fried cauliflower I was used to. Our recipe called for it to be par-boiled, dusted with flour, dipped in egg and bread crumbs, then deep-fried in a pot of oil.

Grandma Wargo bore eight children. They all regarded her highly and treated her with deep respect. The kitchen was a warm and friendly place. We grandkids had the job of stocking the wood box. I enjoyed it and was proud to carry in a large armload of wood. I liked seeing the box go from empty to stacked higher than the sides. I wonder how my mother felt when I'd tell her that Grandma's scrambled eggs cooked on the wood stove tasted better than hers. I think carrying in the wood made the food taste better!

My Father's Heritage

At the Hydeville Mill, Susan met another worker, Domenico Sartori. Susan was 23 years old and Domenico was 33. He, too, had gone into the woolen mill just out of eighth grade.

Domenico Sartori was the second oldest of eight children, his sister Emelia being the oldest. His father, Lorenzo Luigi Sartori, also started off in the woolen mills in Rockville, Connecticut, when he first came to America from the Tyrol of northern Italy.

Lorenzo's family, as well as others, had hard times in Italy as there was no work. He was a second son and would not inherit his father's holdings in the mountain village of Por, Trento, Italy. The village is in the Italian Alps and was part of Austria before World War I. Lorenzo had blue eyes and a red mustache in his younger years. I only knew him as a little man with white hair.

Many Italians came to America in the 1880's, leaving from the port at Genoa. Domenico's mother, Annetta Argenta Sartori, and her family came to America at this time. Lorenzo and Annetta met when Annetta came to Lorenzo's home to work as a domestic in his father's house.

Grandpa Lorenzo was very frugal and saved his money to buy 160 acres of farmland in Staffordville and Union, Connecticut. Originally called Ferry Farm by the previous owners, this 160 acres of land became the "upper farm" where my father and his siblings grew up. The lower farm was purchased later.

The children probably felt isolated on the upper farm, which lay three miles outside the town along a dirt road. They helped with the farm, haying, caring for the cows, gathering grapes, mushrooms, fruit, and making wine. They lived like many farmers do, largely off the land and from the garden. Grandmother Annetta died of consumption, or something like it, when Domenico was 25 years old. She was sorely missed. Her children always spoke so lovingly of her, honoring her memory. The youngest living sibling, my Aunt Eva, was only fifteen years old at her passing.

The Stories Join

Susan and Domenico married in May of 1931. They wanted children very much. Both were working, but would be happy to have Susan conceive and be a stay-at-home mother to rear their children. It was 1938 before their first, Anita Marie, was born. Three and a half years later, in 1942, Elizabeth Ann (that's me) came along. The third and last, Lois Jean, came in 1945. The family was complete because Dr. Shiavetti concluded that with three cesarean births, Susan could not have any more children. He tied her tubes.

During the hurricane and subsequent "flood of '38", Susan and Domenico were living in Stafford Hollow, an area of lower elevation than its surroundings. During the actual flooding, with the hollow already submerged in run-off from the pond and rain still coming, they made their way up Pinney Hill to Echo Farm, a mile or two away. Dad carried the baby, Anita, and Mom carried the baby bottles as they struggled around and over fallen trees that had come down during the hurricane. Much later while telling us girls the story, Mother would exclaim that when they finally arrived at the Wargo Farm, they realized in their haste they'd forgotten the nipples for the baby bottles!

Three and a half years later when I came along, Mom had peritonitis and was not able to nurse. Three years later when World War II was still going on and Mom was pregnant with Lois, Dad's age group was called up to fight in the war. Dad was in Manchester, Connecticut at the induction point, getting his shots to go overseas. The men were standing in line in their underwear as the news came over the radio at just that moment. *The war had ended—Japan had just surrendered!* People were running out in the streets, hugging and clapping each other on the back. We collapsed in mirth, picturing Dad running around in his underwear!

Love and loyalty were strong ties. Domenico brought home his paychecks to his wife and didn't stop at taverns along the way, as many men did in those days. Interestingly, Dad had owned and operated a tavern for awhile and prospered enough to buy the yellow house on the square. He also rented two small apartments that were appendages to the house—one to a couple named Vessely and the other to "Scottie," an older man who had a little trouble with alcohol.

The Vesselys were very kind to me in those preschool years. Anita was in school and Mom was involved with a baby needing vigilant care. I wandered over to the Vessely home and they gave me lollipops. They taught me to sing, "You Are My Sunshine." They even called me "Sunshine," probably more for my blond hair than my sunny spirit. Who knows now?

Dad couldn't stand to see the men come into the tavern and drink up their paychecks, knowing they had homes and families depending on them. He closed the tavern and went to work at Pratt and Whitney Aircraft. That would have been good income for the family but he got awfully bad dermatitis on his arms and hands and had to give it up. He went back to the woolen mill as a weaving machine manager where he worked the rest of his life.

Family came first for my mother. She cooked foods that would please Dad yet still be within the economy of a factory worker's paycheck. I especially remember that she prepared two kinds of soup that Dad loved but we kids didn't. We often found ourselves making peanut butter and jelly sandwiches for those meals. Mom always let Dad know that he came first.

Dad paid tribute to Mom one time when he was talking to me. He said "a woman could make or break a man." When I asked what that meant he explained that a woman could take the paycheck that came in the front door and "throw it out the back door," in other words, waste it on frivolous things. Or she could make it do and her man would feel like he was an adequate provider.

Mom encouraged us children in our individuality. When my sisters and I saw things differently, she would point out, "but you are all so different!" She could see each of our points of view and understand us when we did not understand ourselves, or each other.

I especially appreciate that Mom didn't try to dampen my ways or activity in the out-of-doors. Here was a woman who never went swimming herself, never rode a bicycle, and never in her life of ninety years ever wore a pair of slacks! But she supported me in all those activities.

Mom taught us to be independent. All three of us girls went on to be good and productive citizens. My two sisters reared their families, and I went to college and majored in Elementary Education.

When I was in college, Mom wrote me a letter every week. I did the math one time and figured out that it meant purchasing 200 stamps! Her weekly letters continued after I came to Utah. I usually wrote back to her about every other week. Mom always included cartoons and quips, which I would post on the bulletin board in the dorm. She entertained more people than she realized. Girls stopped to chuckle over her well-chosen cartoons and were also grateful to my mother!

Mother's grandchildren loved her dearly and she loved them. Suzanne, a granddaughter, remembers that she and her brother, Robert, teased my mother by untying her apron strings and dashing away, while she pretended to be mad at them.

At the rest home in her last years, Mom was happy to see us, until she didn't recognize us anymore. On one of my last visits when she still knew who I was, she said: "Oh, Liz is here! I've got to thaw some meat out of the freezer." She was always serving someone.

Mom taught us some valuable lessons with her service, and always by example. She kept a file of papers, maps, and clippings as aids in research for our school reports. The lesson of the value of education came through to me.

Mother taught herself to paint with oils. She had artistic talent which didn't get much encouragement or training. If she had not been sent off to the factory, she would have had an illustrious high school career as she had a desire and talent for art, read voraciously, and had a mind for figures and economy. She used to practice her painting on used light bulbs, really fine designs, and then she'd let us children, when we were very little, put these "ornaments" on the Christmas tree. She let us hang them ourselves, on the lower branches where we could reach, because she didn't think they had as much value as the cheap stuff from the stores. She let us be involved in the holiday preparations.

My sister Lois pointed out to me that our mother taught us that "*things* are not the most important things." Lois has let that guide her mindset on values. She has lovely things and they are fun, but they are just things.

Both of our parents had talents which were not trained or developed. My father had a fine voice and sang with the operas when they came on television, loving the opportunity to use his Italian.

Dad also had a talent for growing green things. Our neighbor, Mr. Simonds, once showed me an old newspaper article about my father and his horticultural skill. Neighbors hired him to do yard work that required skill and a good eye. After he would do the parts that required skill, he often let me mow, doing those parts where mere leg-work would suffice!

Most of the life lessons we learned from our parents were taught by example. There was never one bad word spoken in our home—no swear words or bad language. They also carried no debt, except for $40 left on a new refrigerator at the time of my father's passing.

My father, not having any sons, took me many places with him. I went to hardware stores, cattle auctions, pig slaughterings, and other places that usually were reserved for fathers and sons. Dad made inexpensive toys, like a sled with a barrel stave, a foot and a half of 2 by 4, and an 8" by 10" square board seat. He often loaned me his pocket knife—and I often returned it with a Kleenex wrapped around a finger or other injured part! He took me swimming until I could swim, fishing until I could fish, skating until I could skate. Dad prepared me to do these things alone because he worked so much and so long, usually from 3:00 until 11:00 p.m. He was gone a lot during the week, so Saturdays became quality time.

My sisters were more domestically inclined than I was and preferred to do activities with our mother. I didn't do well indoors because of my hyperactivity, which may have been another factor in the companion travel with my father.

I enjoyed this one-on-one time with my father, always feeling special to him. Interestingly, in talking with my sister Lois, I found that we *all* thought we were Dad's favorite!

3

My Life Continues

As I entered my teen years, I began to show signs of the paths my life would take. I had a great curiosity about the past, where my family came from, who the people were. This curiosity eventually led to an avid interest in genealogy as an adult.

I also began to ponder the mysteries of life, developing an investigative nature that would one day lead me to The Church of Jesus Christ of Latter-day Saints. For now though, I was known as the girl who asked questions incessantly.

Growing Up

When I was in seventh grade, our family moved to Stafford Springs. It was only five miles from Staffordville, but it seemed a world away to me. We owned a new home for the first time since the yellow house in the town square. At the time, it seemed huge to me.

There were many more opportunities for our family in Stafford Springs. More jobs were available. There was a library in town, and I really got into reading. My favorite choices were historical fiction and biographies, but I read everything.

There were also more opportunities for activities for a teenage girl—work, sports (basketball), and school programs like Chorus and Camera Club. I also hiked the trails that began in the woods behind our house.

The trails went up along the ponds and rivers for miles. They probably dated back to the days of the early Native Americans.

I made new friends there. They were chosen quite carefully—or maybe I just got lucky! My friends were loyal, kind, generous, usually adventurous, and they appreciated my qualities. My parents approved of all my friends too, which spoke well of my friends.

One new friend, Linda DeTora, and I collected small libraries of our own and traded books with each other. My small but growing collection was purchased with my meager paper delivery allowance.

My adventurous friend, Wendy Shrier, spent a lot of time outdoors. We biked and rode horses, boated and kayaked. We explored every corner of the pond, right to the edge of the dam. The kayak was named the *Wendy-Bet.* I named the boat *The Sleuth*, but when others went out in it they called it *The Sieve*. My father taught me to caulk it, but apparently it leaked some when it dried out a little.

A Serious and Thoughtful Nature

When Wendy and I rode our bikes, we often visited old and somewhat obscure Revolutionary War and Civil War cemeteries. We loved to read the inscriptions on the stones. I was very aware that these people were indeed people, not just a name on stone. They had lived interesting lives and they belonged to somebody.

When I went up to Echo Farm, the Wargo family farm, I would bike or hike the three miles to get there, and sometimes think deep thoughts along the way. One question I thought about a lot was, *How can I thank God that I don't have some of the severe health issues I see in others?*

Although I had my own health struggles, I was not blind or deaf. I wasn't lame and I didn't have palsy or some of the other diseases that I'd seen or read about. At the age of 12 and 13, the only answer I could come up with was that a person like me needed to help those who had challenges of any kind. Helping others just might be an adequate "thank you" to God.

When I visited with Grandpa Wargo, I asked him questions about my ancestors—*How I was related to so-and-so? Why did Great-Grandma Wargo, his mother, go back to Europe after the war? Why did the family settle in Upper Lehigh, Pennsylvania first? Why did they come to Connecticut later?*

Grandpa was a widower by then. I would walk up to the farm in winter or get a ride from my mother. I'd clean his house and then we would sit and talk or play Cribbage with a board and little pegs. I relished those times of learning about my family. There were always questions to lead the discussion.

Once I asked Mom why relatives weren't visiting Uncle Paul, one of her brothers. She told me it was because he got into trouble when he was young and went to prison. Grandma lost a number of friends.

I replied, "Mom, she just found out who her real friends were." I count that as real wisdom on my part.

When he got out of prison, Uncle Paul opened a furniture shop at Grandpa's farm. He made beautiful things. Mom had received two of his lamps of two-toned, light and dark wood. I visited him a lot in his shop and asked lots of questions.

Did he wear black and white stripes in prison?

No, chinos.

Did he play any sports there?

No, just exercises, mostly, and there was no swimming pool.

Uncle Paul couldn't swim. One year, he asked me to go with him to swim at State Line Pond. He learned to swim by watching me. He loved the water and he was thinking about buying a boat, but about that time he met and married Aunt Sophie, whose first husband had died. She had two children from that marriage and she and Uncle Paul had six more children together. He built a big home for them on a farm when I was 17 years old. I actually helped with the house-building on Saturdays.

One time I discovered that Uncle Paul and Aunt Sophie liked the card game, Pinochle. I knew that Mom and Grandpa liked to play Pinochle, too. I invited them to come down that night and play cards together. They demurred because they hadn't ever been in our home and felt shy. They seemed to think Mom would not want them to visit.

I told them that when I got home I'd ask Mom if it was okay and I'd call them on the phone one way or the other.

When I got home I asked Mom if Uncle Paul and Aunt Sophie would be welcome to come play cards in our home.

She didn't say anything for several of minutes. Finally, I said, "If you don't say 'No' in the next two minutes, I'm going to invite them."

Mom didn't say a word for a minute or two. I called Uncle Paul and said, "Come ahead!"

Over the years, things changed and everyone got along well. Mom, Grandpa, Uncle Paul and Aunt Sophie played cards nearly every Friday night—girls against the guys.

Even at that young age, family was so very important to me!

One other earlier indication of the path my life would take came in high school when my English teacher let us choose our own subjects to research and write about. I always chose Meso-American Archaeology. My early interest in that time period later piqued my curiosity when presented with the Book of Mormon.

Challenges to Blessings

Yet another challenge in my life was getting my growth early. Every time we went shoe shopping I was a half to a whole size larger. By high school my feet were size 10. In college, they would be size 11 with only one other young woman having feet larger than me! Still later I would wear a size 12.

As a teen, it was hard to find a size 10 for girls. We went to four stores in the city of Springfield, Massachusetts before finding a girl's shoe that fit. As may be imagined, there was generally very little choice in style or color at that size. I had to take whatever they had in stock.

This was always traumatic for me. With each store we visited, I felt more and more sorry for myself—one store, two stores, three stores—and the tears were beginning to shine in my eyes. My older sister sometimes chanted, "Herring boxes without topses; sandals were for Clementine." I think sometimes I cried.

This pattern went on for some time, leaving me sad and angry. Then one day somewhere near the end of sophomore year, our English teacher, Mr. Aloysius Ahearn, read something from an old Persian proverb to us: "I cried because I had no shoes until I saw a man who had no feet."

The very next weekend, I found myself on a shoe shopping trip to the city, driving along block after block, looking for shoes large enough for me. The pattern was once again beginning to repeat: two stores already, the Clementine ditty, and the eyes becoming moist.

I happened to look out the car window. There was a man, short and stunted, wearing an elevated shoe and walking with a halting limp. I watched as he made his way in a jerking fashion, along the sidewalk.

Suddenly Mr. Ahearn's quote hit like a blast! I realized in one quick moment how ungrateful I'd been. I had two good feet that took me everywhere I wanted to go. I could go so many places and do so many things on my two feet.

I had been so ungrateful! I have heard it said that two people can have the exact same experience and come away with two entirely different feelings and conclusions. On this day, it felt like in one instant I changed from being an ungrateful person, filled with anger and self-pity, to a completely different person, with a brand new attitude of gratitude.

From that point on, this dramatic change has continued with me. I never again felt sorry for myself. I felt only a deep, deep gratitude for my many blessings. Much, much later, my favorite skiing date, Ken, teased me about having feet the same size as he, while he was lacing my ski boots for me. I just laughed and enjoyed the company.

Another life-changing epiphany occurred around the same time. This time my Dad was tremendously inspired and made a huge difference for good and forever—for which I have ever been and ever will be grateful.

By sophomore year in high school, I was floundering. Dad could see I was maturing rather slowly, due to low self-esteem and the hyperactivity that also took a toll. I was the youngest student in my class, as I had started first grade at five years old. I had also fallen into a rut in my education, choosing to follow my sister's path in a secretarial emphasis in which I had little interest. I played baseball on the street with younger kids and got C's and B's. My father knew I could do much better.

One day, Dad took me aside and said, "Why don't you think about going to college?"

My quick reply, "Aw, Dad, we're too poor and I'm too dumb!" I obviously had some issues with self-esteem and self-worth!

Dad calmly answered my outburst by telling me I was not dumb and if I could get into college, he'd see that I got to stay there financially. He suggested that I go down to the school office the next day and ask for my I.Q. score. We were both naïve enough to think they would tell me.

The next day I dutifully and bravely asked Miss Louise Brunell, the Assistant Principal, what my I.Q. was. Miss Brunell smiled kindly at me and said, "I'm not allowed to tell you your I.Q. but I can tell you that in your class you are 24th for grades and 7th for intelligence!"

We had 79 people in my graduating class. I nearly fainted! I could have told you in a minute 25 people whom I was sure had much higher intelligence than I. I was amazed. I had a brain! Who would have thought? I couldn't wait to tell my Dad.

After my change of heart, I set new goals at the end of sophomore year. I acquired new friends who were age-appropriate and I was very happy. My parents must have been pleased with me, though it wasn't our way to say so. My mother told my neighbor, Dorothy, that I was the most "tractable of her girls." Dorothy repeated this to me and I lived on that compliment for months!

My dearest friend at the time, and still one of my dearest friends now, was Alva Panciera. She pointed me in good directions. We doubled-dated to our Junior Prom. I worked on decorations for the prom but did not expect to go. However, my sister, Anita, got me an escort for that evening and I had a good time.

For my junior and senior years, I switched to college prep courses. I took two Algebra classes, two Latin classes, Chemistry, and several other difficult classes. I got A's and a few B's and became known for my tenacity to seek an A in Mrs. Senechall's Algebra classes. I remember my Mom and Dad looking at my Algebra, Latin and Chemistry books with awe.

Alva and two other friends, Diane Scussell and Susie Cayhill, and I took many rides in Alva's father's green and white Buick. We talked and sang a lot of songs. Alva could harmonize really well, so we always sounded pretty good.

Alva won my parents' hearts big time. If Alva was going, then Mom and Dad were amenable to all our plans. This gives a clue to her character and personality. After graduation, Alva and I, and four other friends, went to Cape Cod for a week's vacation and a wonderful time. At the time, I had what I thought was the best time of my life!

I Go To College

I determined that I was happiest working with children and so Elementary Education was my choice of a major at Central Connecticut State College in New Britain, Connecticut. It took me a whole semester to adjust to being away from home. I got so homesick, I was nearly physically sick. My grades were low when my report came. Dad simply said he knew I'd done the best I could. Ouch!

I got that semester behind me and by second semester, the whole scene got better. I made friends and went out for baseball, basketball, and field hockey. I made Dean's List. All went well until the fall of sophomore year. Again, Dad was an inspiration to me.

I was coming home from college for weekends to work in a restaurant. One night I was studying at the kitchen table when Dad came home from work. It was 11:30 p.m. Mom and my 15-year-old sister had already gone to bed. Dad sat down at the table with a cup of coffee to wind down from the day. We were talking about this and that, and my current concern with morals and religion came up. Not connecting with the seven-year-old's incident at church, I asked him, "Dad, how come you don't go to church?" I could cut to the chase with him, and I did.

He said, "I just can't believe that this [meaning Catholicism] is the one true church." He had thought about it, perhaps read some too, and came to that conclusion on his own and for himself. "All I can do for now is live the Golden Rule."

I repeated the rule aloud. "Do unto others as you would have them do unto you." I exclaimed, "But Dad, that allows too much!"

At school there were decisions to be made of a moral and immoral nature. My roommates were taking the liberal, worldly side and making it sound awfully attractive and exciting. I knew what they were doing was wrong but I was afraid I might have weakened over time

"What do you mean?" he asked.

"I could be having premarital sex with someone," I replied. "I'd be 'doing unto him' what I'd want him doing unto me! The Golden Rule doesn't cover everything!"

Dad expounded on the Golden Rule and on my situation. In his opinion, it *did* cover everything, because it could harm unborn children, and hurt my parents and others who expected so much better from me. Just as I would not want to be hurt and disappointed by those I loved, I should not hurt and disappoint those who loved me. I saw that it did indeed cover everything. Dad actually said more, and said it more eloquently. I don't remember all of it, but I went back to school renewed and with my values reinforced against an atmosphere that was daunting.

My father died about three months later of a heart attack in his sleep on January 2nd, the day before my 19th birthday, sophomore year. I was so grateful for his help, guidance, and the inspiration he'd passed on to me those last three months of his life.

A few weeks before he passed on, I was home for the weekend and asked my Dad to come with me to pick up a pair of scarpèts I had ordered from an old Italian woman in Stafford Springs. Scarpèt are traditionally velvet slippers that young Italian girls wore as a dowry on their wedding day but in America, we wear them at any time. These lovely slippers were hand-made by the older immigrants. The woman who was making my scarpèt didn't speak English; I couldn't speak Italian. When I ordered them, I'd used motions to communicate. I traced my foot on a piece of paper, pointed to something red to indicate the desired color, then pointed to the days on the calendar to know when I should come back to pick them up.

When it came time to pay for the scarpèt, I realized I was in deeper than I could handle. I told Dad I needed him to come when I picked up the slippers. He was thrilled because I needed his seldom-used Italian. I needed him in a *real* way, not just to pay the bills and the usual things that dads do. He and the Italian woman both enjoyed the visit. Although I couldn't understand the words, I could tell that part of the time they were talking about me. They both looked at me and Dad smiled, looking so happy and proud–and he didn't let me pay for the slippers!

Dad and I Go Christmas Shopping

After picking up my scarpèt and leaving the woman's house, Dad suggested we go Christmas shopping for the family before he went to work. What a shock! In my entire life, Mom had always done the Christmas shopping because of Dad's busy schedule. Shopping for Christmas and birthdays was clearly Mom's domain.

We went to Carbone's Jewelry store and Dad bought a silver Cross pen set for me. We picked out a beautiful necklace for Mom and presents for my sisters. Did he somehow know he'd be with us only a few more weeks? I think so. He was inspired to buy presents for his family for our last Christmas together.

There were other indications that he might know his time was short. One day near the end of October, Dad was all dressed up to go to his cousin Angelo's wake. He was going early by himself because he would be at work when the rest of the family went in the evening. He looked quite serious, so I said, "Gee, Dad, you look like you are going to a wake."

"Maybe I'm thinking mine will be the next one," he replied.

It was one of those comments I probably would have forgotten if his passing hadn't happened two months later.

When we had the viewing for my father, my good friends were very supportive, but the hopeless feelings stayed with me a long time. I drew comfort from something my friend, Kathleen Phelps, said at the viewing, that even though we were suffering, he didn't have to.

I used the luggage closet on my hall in the dorm for a crying closet occasionally. I believed I'd never see my dad again. I thought he was lost to me forever! Mother had to deal with her own grief and ours, too. Two years later, my graduation day was a day of mourning because one of Dad's wishes was to see me graduate from college. My mother and Aunt Ethel held me up on either side as I cried uncontrollably at the thought of Dad's absence. Anita threw a party for me after the ceremony.

I threw myself into activities. While at Central, I volunteered at a Catholic Orphanage in Newington, a city nearby. There were about 100 children there and I lead them in games and activities. I also volunteered at the Newington Home for Crippled Children, playing games and leading limited physical activities. At the time there were mostly little boys there. They all had Legg Perthes Disease, a degenerative disease of the hip that occurs only in children. They scooted around on little boards with small wheels on them. When they were in their beds the boys became remarkably adept at catching a ball and passing it back to me.

I Begin My Life's Career

I began teaching fourth grade at Lindon Elementary in Lindon, Connecticut, which is part of the Rockville School District. I lived with my mother and drove a half hour each way. Three very wonderful years passed quickly with much joy and success. The love of the children and their families blessed my life.

During those years I taught archery at a Girl Scout summer camp, coached a girls' softball team, worked as an advisor to some Senior Girl Scouts, and was the leader of three troops of Junior Catholic Daughters. I spent a week camping with the oldest girls at a cabin on the lake. We organized all three troops to make, collect and repair gifts for the children at the orphanage where I'd spent many volunteer hours during college in New Britain. We tossed a Christmas tree on top of the truckload that we delivered. We also "adopted" a couple of families for Christmas and delivered presents to them.

My mother, Grandpa Wargo, and I lived in my mother's house during those years. My sisters were married and I was thrilled to be the aunt of a four-year-old and two new babies. I also appreciated this time with my Mom to talk, reminisce, and grow closer. As I shared my experiences with her, she told me of our history, drawing from her memories.

4

A Call to the West

After three years of teaching in Connecticut, my mother began receiving Social Security. I was feeling quite restless and wanted to see the west. When I'd told my mother where I wanted to go, she said, "Must you go so far?"

I looked at a map of the west and narrowed my options to two—Tucson, Arizona and Salt Lake City, Utah. I checked and the universities in those two cities had Archaeology and Anthropology majors and I had the idea in mind to get a Masters degree.

I called the Salt Lake City School District first and they offered me a job, ten days before the first day of school—sight unseen, no transcripts, no grades. I would be teaching sixth grade in eleven days!

What's a Mormon?

I cleared up my affairs in the east in three days, saying good-by to friends and packing as fast as I could. Barbara Hearn, my neighbor asked, "Where will you be teaching this year, Liz?"

"Salt Lake City, Utah," I answered.

"That's where the Mormons are," said Barbara.

"I wonder what they're like," I mused. I'd never heard the word 'Mormon' before.

It took me seven days to cross the country in my little MGB sports car. Mom wanted me to call her every night while I was on the road, to tell her where I was and to reassure her that I was all right. I thought she'd like to talk to someone else besides myself and so I decided to stop and visit relatives along the way where I could.

The first night out, I stopped in Pennsylvania where Mom's cousin, Gabriel, was a monk in a monastery. They visited on the phone awhile. When Gabriel and I talked about my going to Salt Lake City to teach, he was not as naïve as I was. He got out a huge directory of all the Catholic churches in the United States. He wrote down the names and addresses of five churches in the Salt Lake Valley and reminded me to be sure to live near one of them.

Then he said, "Say, you are 24 years old and not married yet. I'm going to pray that you become a sister!" Apparently he prayed hard and his prayers were answered in the affirmative, because I've been called 'Sister Sartori' many times!

The last relatives Mom got to talk to were an aunt and uncle living in Chicago. After that, I was on my own—no more relatives between there and Utah.

I stopped in Wyoming one night, and while filling the car with gas I asked an attendant to check the oil and water while I went to the restroom. He said he did, but the next morning I ran out of both oil and water. The car came to a smoking stop. My car and I were in big trouble!

I started hiking to a building I saw on the horizon to seek help. Back east that would have been a 15 minute walk, but two hours later the building appeared no closer than when I'd started!

A semi truck came along and the truck driver offered me a ride. He was startled to think I had intended to walk to "that building up ahead." We drove a few minutes at highway speed and arrived at a boarded up old motel. The driver said he'd wait while I checked to see if anyone was around. I crossed the median and circled the whole complex and found no one. I raised my hand to the truck driver to stop and wait for me. He must have thought I was waving goodbye because he pulled away and continued on.

I was dismayed to think of that long walk back to my car, but I started out. After a little while, three men came by in a pick-up truck. They were wearing cowboy boots and their belts had big buckles on them. This was how I thought everyone in the west would look!

The men drove me to a farmhouse behind some sand hills. I had thought there wasn't a living thing out there; luckily I was very wrong! I called Triple A from the farmhouse and they came and towed my car into Cheyenne. A kind woman, the shop owner's wife, got me a plane ticket to Denver and a jet to Salt Lake, because they would need to order parts for my car which needed a lot of attention. This woman was the first Mormon I'd ever met.

I arrived at the Salt Lake Airport, not knowing where to go or what to do next. The sun was sinking behind the Oquirrh Range. A kind officer from United Airlines got me a cab to go into the city and suggested I go to the YWCA. He was a Mormon. So was the cab driver who explained the layout of the city to me. He described the grid with the four cardinal directions, measured from the Salt Lake Temple. I would later become the president of the residents at the YWCA—60 women, ages 18 and up.

The next morning I took the wrong bus. The driver took care to get me on the right bus. He was a Mormon. I got to the Salt Lake City School District meeting to honor my contract.

Just a few minutes late, I took a seat on the aisle. At the conclusion of the meeting, the superintendent told us to have a good lunch, a good afternoon meeting at our respective schools, and a wonderful year. I turned to the woman sitting next to me and exclaimed, "I don't know where my school is, and I don't know where to go for lunch!"

She introduced herself, saying, "I'll take you to lunch and I'll take you to your school!" I introduced myself and thanked her.

We walked into the restaurant and on the counter were some bright blue books with a gold figure on them. "Book of Mormon," I read out loud. "I ought to read that; some of my students may be Mormon."

I can't imagine what this wonderful young woman thought when she heard that. She took me to Edison Elementary, all the way across town on the west side, before going back in the opposite direction to her school. She was a Mormon also.

I got to my meeting just as the principal, Mr. Nicholl (pronounced Nih-KOLL) was saying, "Emily has been in Spain but will be coming into the airport tonight, and as for Elizabeth Sartori, I don't know where she is. She called from Cheyenne, Wyoming with car problems."

"Here I am," I said, and all eyes turned in my direction.

This good man, Mr. Frank Nicholl, introduced me and asked a few questions. After being apprised of my situation, he got me a ride to school every day for two weeks. Later, when he found out I was low on money due to airplane fares, he came to my classroom with an envelope that had $100 cash in it. He told me not to worry about paying it back until I could comfortably do so, and with no interest. A savior in a suit in tie! Yes, he was also a Mormon.

One day, some time after the school year began, one of my students said she had a headache. I sent her down to the office because I did not know the Utah laws for dispensing medicine in school. She came back and sat down and I didn't think any more of it.

A little while later, Alice, our secretary, came into my classroom and placed a couple of aspirin on my desk. "You asked for aspirin," she said.

"Yes," I replied, "but my student was the one with the headache."

"Oh, don't tell Mr. Nicholl," Alice said. "He thought *you* had a headache. We were out of aspirin, so he went and got some for you."

Many more good deeds came from this man over the school year.

The first week of school had gone by and the following week we had a faculty welcome-back-to-school party, up in The Avenues at the lovely home of one of our teachers. At one point I was searching around for an ashtray and puzzled that I could not find one. I went to the kitchen to ask our busy hostess where I could find one. She told me she didn't have any, then after a slight pause, she reached up in a cupboard and said, "Will this do?"

She held a beautiful crystal saucer in her hand. I was dumbfounded and exclaimed, "It's too beautiful. I'll just go out in the backyard."

She was inspired, I think. I would soon find out that only one other teacher in the school besides myself was a smoker.

The next week another teacher had another back-to-school party for us in her home. By this time I had decided you probably shouldn't smoke in front of Mormons, but perhaps someplace nearby would be okay, so I went downstairs to the den.

I was drawn to the bookshelves, as always. Right away I noticed one book, older, with a faded green canvas-like cover. I pulled it off the shelf and it fell open to a written description of people walking toward the Rocky Mountains with packs on their backs. I saw a vision of what I was reading! The packs looked like the ones you see in cartoons with a scarf or kerchief on a stick and held over the shoulder with a hastily-tied knot. There were many, many women and some children, but almost no men. I knew I was reading truth!

The next week a little sixth-grader, Vicki Bills, stopped me as she was going out to recess. "My little brother is being baptized on Saturday," she informed me.

"Oh, what will they name him?" I asked.

Vicki looked at me—and looked at me—and said with a puzzled expression, "He has a name. It's Steven. You're not a Mormon, are you?"

"No, dear," I replied.

"Well, in our church, you're baptized when you are eight years old, and every hair and every toe must go completely under the water!"

Right then and there during recess, Vicki grabbed her friend and demonstrated the process by "dunking" her friend in mid-air. Then they taught me "Give Said the Little Stream" and "I Am a Child of God."

This seems a good place to tell you, dear reader, more of my religious background. I grew up a very active Catholic. ("Try harder," I would tell myself.) I thought about becoming a nun when I helped out at the orphanage in Newington, Connecticut. However, it was an older order of nuns, and they weren't accepting new people.

After much thought, I determined this was not what I should do with my life. Though I was definitely into service to others, especially children, life in a nunnery was not for me.

After I moved to Utah, I went to Catholic Mass after school every day for a year. That first summer, I was the manager of a Catholic Family Camp in the Uintah Mountains. We leased twenty cabins on the Ute Reservation along the Uintah River.

Toward the end of the school year at Edison Elementary, I was at mass when Monsignor M. came up to me after the service and asked me to teach in his school the following year. I said yes for two wrong reasons: First, I was proud to be asked. Second, there was a smoking room in the school for the four lay teachers! Over my career, three principals have asked me to teach for them. I was honored and pleased to do so.

I got a marvelous send-off from Edison Elementary. Our principal, Frank Nicholl, and all the teachers presented me with fishing equipment as a goodbye gift. I would miss this great faculty and staff—and especially the children, to whom I'd become very attached. But the change would be a good one. I was moving to a fourth grade class at the new school—my favorite grade to teach—and ultimately, I have to say this change was a necessary experience for my progression.

Teaching at the Catholic elementary school with four nuns and four lay teachers was an eye-opener for me. There were many new rules to get used to: discipline for discipline's sake, never leave your seat, never talk in the lunch room, and many more. There was also the admonition, "Don't let your children out to the lavatory in the morning, they might steal lunches; nor in the afternoon, they might loiter in the hall."

I volunteered to conduct a Physical Education class after school for the seventh and eighth grade girls. We met in the basement of a nearby church. Our girls needed these skills because when they moved to regular high school, they would be with peers who had already been taught these skills. I wanted these girls to feel comfortable with their new classmates.

One day, our basketball gave up the ghost. It was as flat as a chubby pancake. I went to the Mother Superior's office to get a new ball. I had seen her at a sporting goods store the week before so I thought just maybe there would be a new basketball available for us to use. One of the nuns watched as I explained to her that I was looking in the office closet for a ball. She reported me for a suspected attempt to steal from the closet! When the accusation was made known to me, two months before the end of the school year, I asked, "How much notice do you need?!"

"Two weeks," the Mother Superior intoned.

"You've got it," I said. I left two weeks later.

That last Friday before I left, I purposely waited until the bell was about to ring to tell my fourth graders that I wouldn't be back on Monday. They would have a new teacher. The bell was delayed for two minutes for some reason, and some of the children started to cry. It was especially difficult for one boy, Blake Utley. As soon as the students left, I sat at my desk, arms folded, and I cried, too.

On Monday, I walked into the Salt Lake City School District offices and told them I was an elementary teacher who needed a job. There was an opening at a school on the west side of Salt Lake, not far from where I'd taught before at Edison Elementary. A teacher had left her classroom that morning to work in the school's library. I got a job on the spot!

When I showed up in the classroom, the children were angry. They felt their teacher had deserted them and they took it out on me! It took a whole week to win them over and get their attention. I finally made a connection with them when I drew a water wheel on the chalk board during a Social Studies lesson. They really took note as I illustrated how water ran the grain-grinding wheel. After that, they gave me a break.

That year progressed happily. When it ended, I drove back to Connecticut to visit Mom and family.

I Leave Catholicism

The experience at the Catholic school only added to my troubled state of mind when it came to religion. I wondered why I had so much trouble believing some of the teachings. Of particular difficulty to me were the teachings of transubstantiation–the belief that the communion bread becomes the body of Christ–and the teaching of Original Sin–that we are born with sin on our soul because of Mother Eve and Father Adam's transgression.

I wanted to believe in the religion of my family, so I told myself, "I must try harder!" I tried. I tried very hard. I attended mass regularly. I was involved with the Catholic Family Camp, Ecumenical meetings with the Protestants, and many other activities. When I was called upon to teach concepts that troubled me to young Catholic students, I did. I obeyed and honored my contract but I had no heart for it. I didn't have a testimony of Catholicism, although I would not have used those words to describe my feelings back then.

I was confused. I was strongly Christian and I had a testimony of the Living Lord. But when I considered switching from Catholicism to a different Christian denomination, I thought, "All the Christian churches are off-shoots of Catholicism. How could they be any more true than what I have now?"

For six months, I searched for something to resonate with me. In addition to traditional studies, I read books on parapsychology, psychic phenomena, and other aberrations of spiritual dimension. I charted my own astrology. I planned to meet with a woman who would conduct a séance to consult with a spiritual guide. I had a friend at the University of Utah who had a friend that would get me some LSD to help me "explore my mind," if I'd like to do so. Fortunately, at the last minute, I was saved from investigating some of these more dangerous spiritual alternatives.

As analogy to my experience, I can see a small child crawling vigorously toward a cliff, unaware of the potential harm ahead of her. At the last moment, the hand of a loving Father pulls the child back from the abyss! That child was me! I have cried when thinking back on what could have become of me if I'd continued on in the direction I was going and remembering the power of my rescue.

I was in the midst of this search when I went back to Connecticut for a visit. I could relate to the author, Thomas Wolff, when he said, "You can't go home, but I was trying anyway."

Mom could tell I was troubled but didn't know how to help. I didn't say much. She chalked it up to "those nuns" who had falsely accused me of stealing. I'm sure she felt helpless. She'd always been there for us, but she couldn't shake my mood.

One incident occurred during that visit that shook us both up. I had left a lit cigarette on the edge of a piece of furniture. Mom discovered it when it had burned down close to the edge. She imagined what could have happened had she not noticed it and her voice was filled with emotion when she exclaimed, "Which child would I have to decide to carry out first?!" She wasn't very big or strong, and she had two grandchildren there. It was a sobering thought. I was chagrined that I had caused my mother such distress. I didn't know what to say, and I felt ashamed.

Mom shared her opinion of smoking with us. We knew she thought it was a bad habit and had an offensive smell. She seemed to know of its harmful effects, though at that time people weren't as aware of the physical consequences, like we are today. She shared her thoughts in a way that did not hurt my feelings or cause me to feel attacked; she just wanted me to think about what I might be doing to myself and others.

I'm not sure why I started smoking. I first began smoking at the beginning of sophomore year of college. My Dad wanted to convince me to quit because he knew how "hooked" he was, having smoked for 45 years. He couldn't tell me not to smoke when he himself did it, so he decided to quit before talking to me. He went out in the yard and mowed the lawn furiously, then came into the house and literally sucked down a quart of milk. He went outside again and rolled the whole backyard lawn with a heavy cement-filled cylinder roller for over an hour. Then came back inside and sucked down another quart of milk. (I should add here, he never drank milk that I had ever observed.) By this time he was perspiring profusely and looking ill at ease. He was experiencing withdrawal. He lasted half a day and went back to his cigarettes.

I so admire his desire to deal with the "mote in his own eye" before talking to me. I continued to smoke for another eight years. It is embarrassing how I failed to realize the obvious lesson there, even though Dad didn't say anything I had ample evidence of the obvious harm that could result from continuing on with this habit.

At the end of that summer, I planned to return to Utah to start a Masters program in Archaeology and Anthropology. Unfortunately, I got back a too late to get into school. I didn't want to leave a class of students in the middle of the year again–that had been too painful the year before. I determined to work at something until I could sign up for university studies in January.

The director of the Catholic family camp where I'd worked the previous summer got me a job at a motel. I replaced a girl who had been working there for the summer, Virginia Stanton. She would teach me to work the front desk as she was going back to some place called "BYU". Virginia was bright, cheerful, friendly, and a good teacher.

Not many days later, Virginia came to work wearing a lovely blue dress. When I complimented her on it, she told me she had made it herself. I exclaimed over this and told her of the trouble I was having sewing on a collar for the suit jacket I was working on. She invited me to come to her Aunt Chloe's, where she was staying, and sew with her.

Virginia explained that she lived with her widowed mother in Park City, but stayed at Aunt Chloe's during the week to be closer to her job at the motel. We sewed together and I made progress.

During our conversation, Virginia could see that I was confused on the subject of religion. She asked me why I was disenchanted with my religion. I told her there were too many things I could not believe although I'd tried very hard.

"Like what?" she asked.

I mentioned the Original Sin concept and said it disturbed me to see the lack of trust that might exist when you believed that. I couldn't believe it.

"We don't believe that either," she said. "What else?"

"Transubstantiation. I have tried but I just can't believe the wafer literally becomes the body of Christ. I have had moments of a spiritual 'high' during communion, but I still can not believe this."

Virginia said, "We don't believe that either. We believe that the bread *symbolizes* Christ's body and His sacrifice for us."

"Yes! That's what it should be! What else do you believe?" I asked her.

After a short pause, Virginia answered, "Why don't you come up to Park City this Sunday, and go to church with my Mom and me? Have you ever been to a Mormon Sunday School?"

"No, I haven't."

"Well, would you like to?"

"Well, okay." I answered, thinking I would like to know a little more about what made Virginia the special person I'd sensed her to be.

On Sunday morning I drove up to Park City, a little nervous, but also curious. When Virginia, her mother Evelyn, and I entered the chapel, I was surprised to see people talking with each other. Actually, for two seconds I was appalled! This was behavior in church that I was totally unfamiliar with. My first thought was that people were being irreverent. My second thought, two seconds later, was that these people knew and loved one another! They were not sitting next to strangers. They were sitting with friends. Of course, it would be natural to talk with one another when they came together on Sundays!

After opening exercises, everyone was assigned to classes because it was the first class of the new year. They weren't sure where to put me. Finally, I was invited to attend a class of 17-year-olds. I was 26 years old but someone was truly inspired!

Their new teacher was Brother Dale Durrant. After prayer, he began the class discussion with, "This is a class on the scriptures. What is your favorite scripture?"

No one answered. I certainly didn't know what to say. We all sat there like "bumps on a log" as my mother would have expressed it. Brother Durrant said, "Time is valuable. If you are not going to talk, I will. My favorite scripture is the whole Book of Job."

He went on. "You may recall how my wife and I arrived home on a Friday night, just in time to hear the last cries of our four children as they died in the fire that consumed our home."

I was on the edge of my seat! He went on to describe how he wanted to die. "I saw no reason to go on with life. Life seemed to hold no purpose. I was in despair. I was lost. I didn't want to go on living. And then one day, I came upon the Book of Job."

Brother Durrant bore a beautiful testimony. "The Book of Job strengthened my testimony and made me want to live again, to fulfill all I came to earth to do. After a while my spirit was restored."

"As you all know,," he said, " Sister Durrant and I have four more children. All ten of us plan to be together in the Celestial Kingdom!"

Celestial Kingdom? What was that? Together? Did he mean after they died? I was still on the edge of my seat as he finished his story, consumed with interest and astonishment.

Virginia, Evelyn, and I got back to the Stanton home. They were about to start lunch when I asked, "Virginia, do you have a Book of Job?"

"I think I can find one, Liz," Virginia answered calmly. Definitely an exercise in self-control! She brought her Bible and opened it to the Old Testament. Finding the Book of Job, she handed it to me.

While Virginia and her Mom prepared lunch, I began to read those powerful words about the life and trials of Job—a most worthy and loyal friend to our Heavenly Father. I read all of it, and then flipped pages and found the Book of Ruth. I thought, "A woman! I'll read this one also." Another great story.

I lost all track of time. After lunch, Virginia asked, "Liz, have you ever been to a Mormon Sacrament meeting?"

"Well, no," I replied.

"Would you like to go to one?" Virginia asked.

Thinking about the wonders and revelation of Sunday School, and with the influence of all I'd read, I quickly replied, "Yes, of course!"

I was excited and anticipated what I would hear in the afternoon. I was not to be disappointed. We sang a hymn, "Oh, My Father." How wonderful the words:

> Truth is reason; truth eternal
> Tells me I've a mother there....
> When I lay this mortal by,
> Father, Mother, may I meet you
> In your royal courts on high?

What a thought! What ideas! What a revelation! A mother there? I have a mother there? Of course, how logical! I looked all around me and everyone was singing those startling words. They looked calm enough.

The hymns have power to convert with their melodious renditions of truth and joy. Every hymn I hear raises my level of joy and peace, and willing participation.

When Virginia asked me if I'd like to go to church with them again I told her "Yes!" and the following Sunday I was there again.

After the first invitation from Virginia to come up to Park City, but before I actually went to church with her, another event occurred—evidence of God's perfect timing. An elderly couple came to my door at the boarding house where I lived, looking for Karen Perry. I said they had the wrong door. She lived downstairs and around the corner. They looked discouraged for a brief moment, and then the man said, "Say, would you like to hear about the Gospel of Jesus Christ?"

It seemed like there should have been a light bulb positioned above his head, like in the cartoons, proclaiming a great idea!

"Well, I'll listen," I replied. I guess I learned something from Mom and Dad's good manners. *I shouldn't be rude,* I thought.

"We're missionaries from the Church of Jesus Christ of Latter-day Saints—the Mormons."

"What? I thought missionaries were all nineteen-year-old guys."

They laughed out loud and seemed to think that was one of the funniest things they'd ever heard! They explained that they were Brother Harold and Sister Bertha Olsen from Gunnison, Utah, on a mission in Salt Lake City. They also told me that it was not uncommon to see retired folks on missions for their church.

Sister Olsen asked if I would read the Book of Mormon if they gave it to me.

"Yes, if you are giving it to me," I answered. I wasn't about to buy it, as I'd been confused and searching for almost a year, and more than a little cynical about people who wanted to sell me spiritual knowledge.

Sister Olsen gave me the book and asked when I'd like my first lesson.

"Don't call me. I'll call you," I replied as I wrote their names and phone number in the back of the book.

It was just after their visit that I went to Park City with Virginia the first time. After that incredible Sunday at church in Park City, I started reading a little in the Book of Mormon.

The next Sunday, I went to church with Virginia and Evelyn again. We sang "Come, Come, Ye Saints." That hymn spoke powerfully to my heart. I wrote all the words in the back of my Book of Mormon.

Again, I had a wonderful day with my new-found friends, and returned to Salt Lake City to work on Monday. I called the missionaries and told them I'd been to church in Park City. They were surprised. I invited them to come for a lesson. I told them of my experiences in Park City and shared the stirring story of the Durrants.

The next weekend, I went to church with the Stantons again. Virginia's brother, Jim, and his wife, Bernice, and their children came for the afternoon. Eight-year-old Lloyd answered gospel questions I posed. I was impressed—an eight-year-old in a white shirt and tie had considerable knowledge for his age and the confidence to share it.

After they left, Virginia asked, "Have you ever been to a Mormon fireside, Liz?"

"No, I haven't," I replied, with visions of a fireplace with logs burning in a cozy atmosphere.

"Would you like to go?"

"Sure, when?"

"Tonight."

A couple had gone to the South Seas and brought back slides to show. Lemon meringue pie was served. There was no cozy fireplace. I realized much later that Virginia and I were the only uncoupled couple there. She wanted me to go to every event she was able to take me to!

When we got into my vehicle after the fireside, I took a cigarette out of my purse. I hadn't had one all day. I was surprised I hadn't missed it. Virginia who could have said a lot of things, just said, "Liz, I just can't picture you with a cigarette!"

The very next morning, I had run out of cigarettes. I thought, "Virginia can't picture me with them. I'm going to try to picture me without them." Then I thought, "I ought to see if I can get up in the morning without my cup of coffee. And maybe I'll try to do without afternoon tea. I think I'll try a 'Mormon experiment'—no more piano bars on weekends... I didn't know if my body could adjust to all these changes. I'd just have to see.

After Virginia went back to BYU, which I now knew was Brigham Young University, I was working alone at the desk one afternoon. I was whistling the tune to "Come, Come, Ye Saints" when a group of 25 women came in the door. They laughed as they said my song invited them in, being Latter-day Saints. They were from Las Vegas and had come to Salt Lake to sing for the General Relief Society Conference and the first day of General Conference. There were 400 women altogether in their group, staying in motels and hotels near Temple Square. They were surprised when I told them I'd only heard the song for the first time the week before.

We began writing everyone's names on a piece of paper as we determined who was staying with whom, five to a room. There was a lot of talking and noise as they decided on roommates. I was handing out keys to the groups.

The manager came in just then. She impatiently grabbed the paper from me and wrote down names, quickly assigning groups to particular rooms. Then she told me to help them upstairs with their luggage. When we got upstairs to their floor, the ladies took the list from me and rewrote it to suit themselves. One group asked if we had any more hangers. I asked if they would still be up at ten when I got off work. I could bring them extra hangers then. They said they'd still be up and I went back downstairs.

When I brought the new, updated list back to the desk, the manager became angry. She turned abruptly toward the phone and then thought better of it, and stormed off to her rooms. That night at 10:00 p.m. I was fired! The motel didn't have any hangers, but since I'd promised them, I decided to go upstairs and tell them I could bring them some extras tomorrow, "even though I wasn't scheduled to come in."

I was purposely trying to mislead, when one of the women asked, "Why aren't you scheduled to come in tomorrow?"

Oh, groan, the truth! I had to say I'd been fired. The women worried that it was because of them. "Don't worry, because I don't appreciate the managers anyway. I plan to sign up for substitute teaching." I said.

"Do you like music?" one of the women asked.

"You bet!"

"What are you doing tomorrow?" another woman asked.

"Nothing. I haven't signed up for substitute teaching yet."

"We have a rehearsal tomorrow at the Tabernacle, and we need a ride–"

"Okay," I said. "I'll be here twenty minutes before the hour."

They introduced themselves: Diana Andrus, Toni Frehner, Betty Hendricks, Mardell Olsen, and Viola (Vi) Freshwater. They gave me copies of the music they would be singing, and I left for home–unemployed but happy to be helpful.

When we got to the Tabernacle on Temple Square next morning, I noticed there was only one other person sitting in the congregation's seats. I went over to share my music with her. Donna Buttle had lived in Las Vegas at one time, and was hoping to meet up with some of her old friends there that day. I told her how I happened to be there. She took down my name and address and later sent me *A Marvelous Work and a Wonder* by LeGrand Richards. Inside the book she wrote:

> Dear Liz, we hope this book will help your testimony grow ever-stronger, as you read and recognize the truth even more powerfully. What a choice person you are–and we feel so fortunate to call you our "dear friend". Good luck and God bless you in all your endeavors.
>
> Lovingly, Your friends, Donna and Lynn Buttle and Donnalyn.

We went out to lunch that day after the music practice. I took my new friends to a favorite restaurant before taking them back to the motel I'd been fired from the day before. Vi Freshwater asked, "What are you doing tomorrow, Liz?"

"Well, nothing," I said. "I haven't signed up for substitute teaching yet."

"Well, tomorrow—Wednesday—we sing at General Relief Society Conference. You'd really like that meeting—and we need a ride!"

They were right; it was a marvelous meeting. We went out to dinner again and I brought them back to the motel. With everyone smiling big grins, someone asked again, "What are you doing tomorrow, Liz?"

"Well, nothing. I haven't signed up for substitute teaching yet!" I replied, laughing with everyone.

Then Betty said, "We don't have an assignment tomorrow, so we want to go to the Genealogical Library and work on our Genealogy. And our books are very heavy. And we need a ride!"

"Okay," I agreed.

Thursday morning I went back to the motel and we left for the library, with all of them carrying their books and papers. They sat me down at a table with some white papers, pink papers, and yellow papers, and told me how to fill them out with whatever I knew. Unbeknownst to me, I was beginning to prepare my four-generation sheets. That was my introduction to genealogy. Since then, so much has been accomplished—about 12,000 of my ancestors have had their temple work done!

Again we went out to dinner that Thursday night. On the way back from dinner, Betty Hendricks said, "Would you like to watch the ten o'clock news with us? There's going to be a little segment from the Relief Society Conference and we want to see if we'll be on television."

"I would love to come," I answered.

We went upstairs to watch the news, and sure enough, we saw my friends on the screen, briefly. When the news concluded, we began to talk. I asked questions and they took turns answering and bearing their testimonies to me. The spirit was so strong it was almost tangible!

Finally someone asked, "What time is it, anyway?"

"I bet it's after 10:00," I thought. It was one o'clock in the morning! How the time had flown! These wonderful, loving women had answered all my questions. We all had tears of joy in our eyes.

To relieve this serious moment, someone spoke: "So, what are you doing tomorrow, Liz?"

Of course, we all burst out laughing and I came up with the standard reply: "Nothing, I haven't signed up for substitute teaching yet!" We laughed again.

"Tomorrow is the first session of General Conference, and we are scheduled to sing in the morning. We fly back to Las Vegas tomorrow night. We need a ride to conference, and a ride to the airport afterward."

The next morning I was there, bright and early–very early–for the first session. I waited in line while they went inside. While I was standing in line, I met Lydia Stewart, who became interested in my story.

I was not a member of the Church, and there I was waiting to get into the Tabernacle building. I had brought five of the women from Las Vegas who would be singing at this morning's session. She told me she had not been able to attend the Relief Society Meeting on Wednesday, and she was very pleased that I could tell her about it because she was a Relief Society President in her ward (like a parish). She later sent me the *Articles of Faith* and wrote in it:

> To Elizabeth Sartori, In admiration for you and your sincere interest in the wonderful Gospel of Jesus Christ. From a friend met at General Conference.

When we got inside and seated, I could see my five friends. Two of them came down to where I was seated and brought me a shiny new hymn book. They had all signed it. What a thoughtful gift! I got to sing with everyone during the congregational singing.

After the conference, we went to lunch before the afternoon session. When the afternoon session concluded, the girls got their suitcases and we went to the airport. After bringing them to the airport, I lingered, watching until their plane was in the air. I felt a sudden sense of loneliness. My new-found friends were on their way back home to Las Vegas and their families.

I met with the missionaries again. The first time we met, I'd gone to Park City. The second time we met, I'd been to church in Park City again. The third time we met, I had the rich experiences with my new friends to relate and the new hymn book. By our fourth get-together, I'd received the *Articles of Faith* from Relief Society sister, Lydia Stewart.

Also before their third visit, I had decided to start my "Mormon Experiment" with the Word of Wisdom. I kept it going. I didn't even need to chew gum. It was easy! This from a person who was not able to give cigarettes up for Lent, the Catholic biggy! I didn't miss the piano bar, even though it was very fine live piano music, with a drink or two for the evening—a frequent "date" experience. The fact that I could easily give it all up was both profoundly shocking and exceedingly pleasing.

Years later, I learned why it had been so easy. I had taken Virginia's niece, Evelyn, and some of her high school friends from Provo to General Conference in Salt Lake. On the way back we were discussing the talks, when Evelyn said, "I can remember when we fasted and prayed for you, Liz."

"What? I've never been 'sick nigh unto death'! I exclaimed.

"No, it was when you had those Word of Wisdom problems," Evelyn replied.

Then I knew what had really happened. No wonder I thought it was so easy! Virginia had gone to her mother, her brother and his wife, and all their children—and they were fasting and praying for me! I clearly felt the power of their fasting and prayer, even when I didn't know they were doing it! And it was POWER!

When Brother and Sister Olsen came to teach me the lesson on the Word of Wisdom, they were hemming and hawing, saying things like, "You feel so much better when you obey the Word of Wisdom," and, "You can do so much more. Your health would be better. Cigarettes cost so much..."

"I think you may be right," I said, "since I stopped using those substances, I'm already feeling better physically and spiritually. I've had such good experiences."

Were they ever surprised! I think they were so startled they didn't know what to say. The Olsens skipped that lesson and went on to the next lesson subject.

I missed my friend Virginia, who had gone back to BYU, and I determined to visit her in Provo. I packed a small bag, just in case it became an overnight visit. When I arrived on Saturday mid-afternoon, Virginia was not there. Her roommates said she was cooking dinner for some guys and gave me an address. There were a dozen guys living in that house and they invited me to dinner. (What else could they do?) All the chairs were turned away from the table, and before we sat down to dinner, everyone knelt by their chairs and had prayer. I didn't even know such men existed! That half of humankind immediately became more attractive!

I followed Virginia home and officially met her roommates. She was in the upstairs apartment and there was another apartment downstairs. They were together often, however. I didn't stay overnight but I was invited to come the next weekend with the intent to stay over.

The next Saturday, Virginia asked, "Liz, have you ever been to a Mormon fast and testimony meeting?"

"No, I haven't."

"Would you like to go with us tomorrow morning?"

"I'm up for it; you bet!" By now I knew an invitation from Virginia had to be a good thing!

As we sat in the meeting, people began to take turns standing and speaking. All of a sudden, my heart was thumping in my chest. I thought it was going to fall out on the floor! I said to the girl nearest to me, "Can anyone get up and speak?"

She looked puzzled but she said, "Yes, of course!"

I rose involuntarily from my seat and walked forward. And I spoke. And I cried some. I was sure—sure it was true! I knew! *I knew!* ***I knew!***

I'd been holding back for so long because I wanted to be so sure. The gospel seemed too good to be true at times. I was also concerned because at first I thought the Church was another Protestant church. It is not! It is the Restored Church, restored to the way it had been in the times of the Savior and His apostles.

That was in the fall. In the spring, I was living in Provo. A girl said to me, "You're the one who bore her testimony last fall!"

I didn't know what I'd said at the time; the words were given to me.

We were sitting down to lunch after church. Virginia looked at my watch that had a little blue medal of Mary, the earthly mother of Jesus, attached to it—a common sight in my former church. She asked if I worshiped the medal.

"No," I said. "Truth to tell, I'd forgotten it was on my watch." Then I remembered kissing the one around my neck before going in swimming, and seeing people praying in front of a statue of Mary. "But I can see how you might think so," I added.

"What about the fourth commandment?" Virginia asked.

"Honor thy father and they mother?" I asked. "It's a good one. I'm all for it."

"No, the one about graven images."

"There's no commandment about graven images!" I exclaimed with certainty.

"Yes there is," she insisted.

"Show me," I said.

Virginia got out her Bible and opened it to the Old Testament, Exodus 20:4. I was really surprised. Honor thy father and thy mother is a few verses later. I had been taught the Ten Commandments differently, and the commandment about the graven images was left out. There are differences between the King James Bible, which the Mormons use, and the Duay version, which I'd used as a Catholic.

Then it was Virginia's turn to be surprised. I took the medal off my watch and the one from around my neck and put them in my purse.

Before that weekend, I'd had many wonderful experiences with my friends in Park City and Salt Lake City. During the process of learning about the Church, everything seemed extraordinary, but I did not have that special witness from the Holy Ghost until the fast and testimony meeting. Until then, I would occasionally have thoughts about how my family would take the news that I was considering a new religion. I wondered how they would react and hesitated to tell them. But after that Sunday, once I *knew*, there could be only one course of action.

When I'd first met Harold and Bertha Olsen, they'd asked when I'd like to be baptized. I was shocked to say the least, and I replied, "Don't call me. I'll call you." I actually thought it would never happen, but I was baptized two months from that time.

I was scheduled to be baptized in the Tabernacle font on Temple Square, but when I set the date, the Olsens said the font wouldn't be filled for two more weeks. I was impatient for baptism. I also worried that something might happen to me, like an accident, that would prevent me from being baptized. I was, oh, so careful—home at night before dark, looking both ways twice before crossing the street. I didn't want anything to jeopardize my chance to become a member of the Church of Jesus Christ of Latter-day Saints on October 25th!

I sent a note to my friends in Las Vegas telling them of my upcoming baptism. They sent back a congratulatory telegram. I was baptized by Lenn Roie Wooley, one of the men who lived at the house where I ate dinner that one time in Provo. Six others of those good men sang at my baptismal service, "Oh, That I Were an Angel." Brother Olsen confirmed me. Twelve men placed their hands on my head for that blessing. Virginia's Aunt Chloe had a reception for me afterwards at her home.

I Believe

This book would just be a report of wondrous events if I did not include my feelings of gratitude for the blessings of my life and testify of the truths I know and the knowledge I've acquired.

Many people reading this book are not members of my church, so I would clarify some things here. First, there is a summary of things I know to be true in the Articles of Faith. These are the basic tenets of our religion. Joseph Smith, the first prophet of this Dispensation of the Fullness of Times, wrote a letter to a Mr. Wentworth, the editor and proprietor of the Chicago Democrat, because he had asked Joseph to tell him just what the Mormons believed. It contained these 13 tenets:

1. We believe in God the Eternal Father, and in His Son, Jesus Christ, and in the Holy Ghost.

2. We believe that men will be punished for their own sins, and not for Adam's transgression.

3. We believe that through the Atonement of Christ, all mankind may be saved, by obedience to the laws and ordinances of the Gospel.

4. We believe that the first principles and ordinances of the Gospel are: first, Faith in the Lord Jesus Christ; second, Repentance; third, Laying on of hands for the gift of the Holy Ghost.

5. We believe that a man must be called of God, by prophecy, and by the laying on of hands, by those who are in authority to preach the Gospel and administer in the ordinances thereof.

6. We believe in the same organization that existed in the Primitive Church, viz, apostles, prophets, pastors, teachers, evangelists, etc.

7. We believe in the gift of tongues, prophecy, revelation, visions, healing, interpretation of tongues, etc.

8. We believe the Bible to be the word of God as far as it is translated correctly; we also believe the Book of Mormon (Another Testament of Jesus Christ) to be the word of God.

9. We believe all that God has revealed, all that he does now reveal, and we believe that He will yet reveal many great and important things pertaining to the Kingdom of God.

10. We believe in the literal gathering of Israel and in the restoration of the Ten Tribes; that Zion will be built upon this (the American) continent; that Christ will reign personally upon the earth; and that the earth will be renewed and receive its paradisiacal glory.

11. We claim the privilege of worshipping Almighty God according to the dictates of our own conscience, and allow all ment the same privilege, let them worship how, where, or what they may.
12. We believe in being subject to kings, presidents, rulers, and magistrates, in obeying, honoring, and sustaining the law.
13. We believe in being honest, true, chaste, benevolent, virtuous, and in doing good to all men; indeed, we may say that we follow the admonition of Paul—we believe all things, we hope all things, we have endured many things, and hope to be able to endure all things. If there is anything virtuous, lovely, or of good report or praiseworthy, we seek after these things.

Personally, I know the Gospel—the "good news"—of Jesus Christ is true. I know that Jesus Christ is the Son of God, and that He did indeed die for my sins, and for all of us. He is my personal Savior and the Savior of all mankind.

I know that we lived in the spirit world before coming to Earth. We came to Earth to get our bodies, which we will take up again at the resurrection.

I love my Father in Heaven. I love the Gospel of Jesus Christ. In the Living Christ is all hope, all love, all that is good. I want to be His, forever. I love and appreciate the good people who have influenced my life.

The power and authority of the priesthood are on the Earth today. I have received blessings, with hands placed upon my head by worthy holders of the Melchizedek Priesthood, as has happened in all of the seven dispensations of time. I have experienced renewed strength, restored health, and ceasing pain.

5

After Baptism, What?

When I wrote to my Mom to tell her about my decision to be baptized, she sent a letter right back and asked, "Where have we gone wrong; haven't we always been good examples?"

This was not a ploy or emotional manipulation, she really wanted to know. I was able to answer immediately: "You have never gone wrong, and you were always good examples. That is why I could recognize good when I found it."

There was never any difficulty after that. Her communication and love were always there. I think she was happy to see some of the changes in me. I was more loving and I communicated it better. I stopped smoking, a habit she abhorred.

My Family's Reaction

The first time I went to the temple, there were no shoes my size in the women's clothing section. I wore size 12 remember? I asked Mom if she would go to the unique store in Hartford, to get me white shoes and nylons at the place where she had bought shoes and nylons for me before. I told her they needed to be white, because that's what you wear in the temple. They came, almost by return mail! I was so grateful to her for doing this. She was always very supportive of me–of us, I should say, as my sisters have felt that support, too.

My sister, Lois, was impressed. She said she admired me for doing what I thought I should do. But her first question when I told her of my intention to be baptized was, "You do still believe in Jesus Christ, don't you, Liz?"

"Oh, yes!" I replied. Some may have thought my baptism was another one of 'Liz's larks' and would be a passing thing. On a trip back east to visit Mom, I stopped at Great Uncle John's home in Pennsylvania. Our Mother loved and admired her sweet uncle. I invited him to come with me up to Connecticut to visit Mom. Just before we left, his daughter, Margaret, said, "I'd never hurt my mother the way you've hurt yours." Uncle John prayed his rosary in the back seat of my car as we drove on to Connecticut.

I cried during that trip from Pennsylvania to Connecticut. When we arrived, I said to Mom, "Cousin Margaret said she'd never hurt her Mom the way I've hurt you, and I want you to know there are a lot of things in this world–sniff, sniff, sniff–I'd rather do than hurt you."

I cherish Mom's reply. "Cousin Margaret doesn't know everything!" Mother was a little like Golda, in *Fiddler on the Roof*. I loved her so much at that moment, I felt like falling at her knees and kissing her feet!

Great Uncle John had been polite, but reserved, the whole trip. I went outside a little later to explore my old digs. When I came back in, Uncle John showed considerably more warmth. I think Mom shared what was in her heart with him.

Mom's and Dad's temple work is done. They are sealed to each other for time and all eternity, and I am sealed to them. I am the only one of my siblings who believes I need to be sealed to our parents, but it sure makes me feel good! It was an extraordinary day.

Immersing Myself in the Gospel

I went to Brigham Young University, and began a Masters program in Archaeology and Anthropology. I'd reasoned: "Where can I go to learn as much as I can, as quickly as I can, about my new religion? I know! I'll go to BYU."

I was there two years, including two summers working on Anasazi sites–eight weeks each summer–in Montezuma Canyon between

Blanding and Monticello, Utah. The second summer I had my own site to map and excavate. Every Saturday we took field trips. We studied Keet Seel, Betatikan, Howvenweep, Mesa Verde, Nine Mile Canyon, Hopi Mesa, Canyonlands National Park, Grand Gulch, Comb Wash, and many pueblos and cliff dwellings.

I enjoyed those two years as a student, but I ran out of money and missed the children and the classroom. I went back to teaching Elementary School. Calvin Walker had come down to the Archaeology Summer School and while he was there, asked me to come and teach in his school in Pleasant Grove.

I stayed in the BYU wards another two years, living with students as roommates. I took the total immersion approach to acquiring gospel knowledge. I was a Relief Society teacher, a Young Women's President, and a Relief Society President. When I was called as Relief Society President, President Page suggested I go visit a sister named Roselyn, to see if she should be my second counselor. He also told me I should choose both counselor and a secretary by Sunday.

I hopped on my red Honda motorcycle on Saturday afternoon to go meet Roselyn. Holding my helmet under my arm, I knocked on her door. We chatted a while. Her story was very interesting. I learned that she was a convert–and that she had converted herself! She has gone to an Osmonds concert and learned they were Mormons. Curious, she went to the library and did a little research, read the Book of Mormon, converted herself, and subsequently joined the church. We hit it off quite well, and I asked her if she would like to be our second counselor in Relief Society.

She exclaimed, "My Relief Society President is riding a motorcycle? Count me in!" We were two of a pair, with unique interests. We never held a presidency meeting when Star Trek was on television because Roselyn was a true-blue trekkie!

As a relatively new member of the Church, I didn't know how to go about getting a first counselor and a secretary. It was Saturday night and the bishop wanted names by the next morning. When I prayed to Father in Heaven that night, I suggested that the first two women I met on Sunday morning would be our first counselor and secretary.

The next morning as I came into church, two young women were talking with each other in the foyer. I introduced myself and asked their names. We visited a minute and then I asked them to come to President Page's office with me.

"Good morning, President Page. I'd like you to meet Evelyn Dubins. I believe she would make an excellent first counselor." Then I turned to the other woman. "I'd like you to meet Cathy Itri. She would make a very good Relief Society secretary," I explained.

This was the first they'd heard about their new callings! Later, Evelyn and Cathy told me that they had never met before and weren't quite sure why they were out there talking, instead of going inside for the meeting.

When the callings were officially extended, accepted and sustained, we found we had a converted Catholic Relief Society president, a converted Jewish first counselor, a converted black Baptist second counselor, and a secretary who'd been a Mormon all her life. It was a fabulous year. We grew close and accomplished much. Later, when Roselyn moved on, Kathy Quilter became the second counselor. Evelyn Dubins Robertson, Cathy Itri Lloyd, Kathy Q. Woolf and I are still in contact.

In the regular "home" wards, I have worked 16 years as a Stake Young Women Camp Director–still my favorite job in the Church. I've also worked in Sunday School, Primary, and in the library. Actually, all of these callings were favorites, just for different reasons.

During these years in the BYU wards, I earned a Masters Degree in Education. I also taught school all those years, worked in church callings, and did genealogy. Actually, I'd have to say I was getting my genealogy done, as I had two genealogists working on my research, Trafford Cole for a few years, then Keith Rose.

There have been miracles in doing genealogy work. I stand all amazed when I consider how fortunate I have been to be able to do the work of my kindred dead. While I was still investigating the Church, my father came to me in a dream one night to let me know he was "stopped." I had something to do with him being able to progress and move on from where he was in the Spirit World. I was made to understand that the help involved me, but I didn't understand it at the time. I knew I had seen him and thought, "I must have something to do." I believe he wanted his temple work done.

One day, I was talking with Mom as she was diapering her grandson, my nephew, whom she was tending. I remarked how sad it was that Dad didn't get to see this cute little fellow in this life, born a year after Dad died. She said, with almost a murmur, "Maybe he has."

I was shocked! I could tell this was close, very close, to my Mother's heart. She didn't often share things close to her heart. I held my breath, not daring to breathe or speak and lose this moment. I very quietly replied, "What do you mean?"

"He was standing right there, in back of me, looking over my shoulder at Robert while I was changing him the last time he was here," she said very quietly. I asked if they had spoken and she said she was too frightened to even turn all the way around.

Genealogy, I Am Doing It

One morning, just before leaving for school at Orchard Elementary, I got the strong impression that I should take my little folder of Mom's people's genealogy papers and certificates to school. "To school? What an absurd idea!" I thought. I tried to shrug it off, but the feeling persisted, so I packed it along with my school stuff. It was only the second week of school, and I was very busy. I hardly knew the students, much less any of their parents.

Laurie Castillo and her son, Samuel, my second grader, came in the door early, before others had arrived. I assumed she wanted to discuss her boy—and maybe we did—I can't remember. But what I do remember and will never forget, was that she looked at me strangely and said, "I am going up to the Church Genealogical Library today and I think you should meet me there." Boinnng!!! I stammered that I did, indeed, need to go there. After school was dismissed, I drove up to Salt Lake.

After we met, we went into a room filled with stacks of books on the shelves. I opened my folder on the table to show Laurie the certificates that had come into my hands over the years—a marriage certificate for my mother's parents, naturalization papers, and a few other items. They were printed using a Cyrillic alphabet.

Suddenly Laurie said, "That man over there has got a book open with letters like the ones on your certificates!"

We walked over and found two generations on one line of my ancestors. What a faith-promoting experience that was! My ancestors had a strong desire to be found and to have their work done. I am humbled that they could work through me. I'm not a particularly attentive person, with some ADHD tendencies, yet they were able to give me the message to get up there to Salt Lake and to find that information, on that day and at that time. These people, want their work done!

When I go to the temple, I often get what I call the "joy feeling." I can't stop smiling and I am so happy inside. This feeling often dissipates as I leave the temple grounds. But one Friday night, the feeling stayed with me all the way home. On Saturday afternoon, I visited with my friend, N.V. She "sees" things the most of us don't see. It is her Gift of the Spirit. She said, "Last night I dreamed you were standing at the top of your stairs and all down your stairs there were women dressed in white. They were all looking up at you, smiling. Why did I see that?"

"Oh," I said, "Last night I was baptized for fifty-two of my female ancestors!"

"That's it," she answered, "Last night you had angels in your home!"

One night, as I was "sleeping," a relative who wanted his temple work done came to me. I had overlooked him. He brought a multitude of people him. I was surrounded by the nearly tangible love emanating from them. They left when I started to look for specific people, specific faces.

When I arose in the morning I was still basking in that special love. It was very powerful, and some time before I could bring myself to get on with the day's activities. My relative's work was done not long after.

My genealogist was making a trip to Italy to work for five clients for 17 days. I had a strong desire to go there with him. I asked him to get me a ticket, too. We went to northern Italy in the Tyrol, the Italian Alps, where my grandfather was born, to a tiny village near Trento. It was a cloudy day in February. We saw a little church and not very far from it, a cemetery, with walls about three feet high surrounding it. In the cemetery, there was room for about 175 internments, and every one of them was filled.

In Italy, when a cemetery becomes full, they exhume all the bodies, throw the bones in a pile, and start over again. When we were there, every space was occupied and had a headstone. Every occupant was related to me. My genealogist suggested we do everyone's work–direct line of aunts, uncles, cousins, all the way back–ten years at a time. This would be in keeping with my Patriarchal Blessing which says I have many, many worthy and wonderful ancestors waiting for me to "open the door for them."

I felt "called" by those wonderful ancestors to go to Italy. That 17 day trip caused me to miss eleven or twelve school days–something I'd never done before in my career. I traveled all over Italy, as research was being done for the other four clients. One other client met us in Sicily.

On another trip when I did not go, my genealogist went to Feltre, my grandmother's village, also in the Tyrol. He followed four lines back all the way to the year 1540. Another exciting highlight is that "cousins" have found me, due to my materials at the genealogical library. I also found out that my dearest friend from high school is actually my 4th cousin!

In the book *The Hiding Place*, Corrie Ten Boom says, "There is a joyous journey which each of God's children sooner or later sets out on. And Jans, some must go to their Father empty-handed, but you will run to him with hands full!" That is how I feel about doing genealogy work. I will be able to run to my Father with hands full.

My Life Is Preserved

My life has been preserved many times. I think it was so I could do this genealogical work. Before I ever left Connecticut, while on vacation with friends at Cape Cod Bay, I was carried out to sea in a seven-foot plywood rowboat. I saw a shipwreck, grounded out in the bay. On the shore were two boys with their boat. I asked if I could use it to row out to the wreck. They agreed, and I went to work with a will. (Did I say ADHD comes with a tendency to impulsivity and spontaneity?) I didn't realize the shipwreck was three miles out. That is a long way in a small boat! Soon the water got choppy. My oars kept trying to jump out of the oarlocks. Eventually, I pulled the oars in, waiting for the end when I would fall asleep and fall overboard or capsize.

A larger fishing boat came along and the skipper leaned over the rail of the boat, clearly puzzled and somewhat alarmed, and asked what I might be doing out there. I told him I'd wanted to go out to the wreck but the oars kept jumping out of the oarlocks. He told me the tide was going out, I wouldn't be able to get back in until 5:00 a.m.!

Then he thought a moment and said he could tow me in toward shore. When he got close enough that he feared running aground, I'd have to row on my own the rest of the way. Rowing one-third of the way back to shore wasn't quite so hard.

The breeze had sent me like a human sail down the beach. I had to walk a mile to get back to where I had taken off. The boys were happy to see their boat again. My friends, Alva and Ron, had been quite worried and were now overjoyed to see me alive and well. They had been about to call the Coast Guard! It was then they told me that the ship was put there on purpose by the Air Force, to be used as a target for their airplanes. If the fishing boat hadn't come along, I might have become target bait for the Air Force.

When I first came to BYU, I didn't have a car. I'd heard there was someone up at the Genealogical Library who could help with Slovakian and Hungarian records. One day when I didn't have any classes, I decided to ride my bike up there. I rode the 40+ miles to Salt Lake. Once there, the genealogy helper guided me through some of what I needed to know. This took the whole of the day and it was dusk when I left the library. I decided to go over to the bus depot and splurge for a bus ticket to Provo. I'd have them toss my bike in the luggage hold.

They told me they didn't take bicycles, unless they were still in the box. I left on my bike for a long, cool, dark ride home. I was riding up the hill near the point of the mountain by the state prison, walking at that point, when a truck pulled up about a block's distance from me on the side of the highway. I thought, "If they'll let me, I'll throw my bike and me in the truck bed and ask to be let off at a Provo exit."

At that moment I got what I call "the dark feeling." I didn't feel good at all about what was up ahead. I said a quick prayer that whatever happened I would be able to handle it.

As I came up alongside the truck, a man suddenly opened the driver's side door. I had to stop for a moment. He asked me something like, what was I doing out there on a highway in the dark alone.

Out of the corner of my eye, I saw the other man had quietly gotten out on the his side of the car and was walking, crouched down, along the passenger side.

I yelled, "Well, gotta be going!" I leapt out and around the door, onto my bicycle, and got up the rest of the hill fast, adrenaline supplying me with Olympian energy! I took the first exit into Lehi and determined to take my way home through the towns along the way!

Yet another time when I was still at BYU, I met a group of girls from the Moron Colonies of Mexico. We were all on a ward basketball team and they were good ball players. The girls had been playing full-court basketball long before we did in the United States. We won all our games in our own stake and then the stakes play-offs. One girl's family had just moved up to Mapleton from Colonia Juarez. Her high school-aged sister,

Irva Lee, missed her friends and classmates that were graduating that year in the colonies. They told me stories of life there and of miracles that had occurred. I longed to see their homeland.

Irva Lee, her friend and I left in my trusty Volkswagon to go see this marvelous place with such rich history. After we crossed the border, we travelled on narrow dirt roads. A huge, blinding sandstorm stopped us in our tracks. I pulled over onto the very edge of the road, because none of us could see anything. Looking at the windshield was like looking at a piece of sandpaper.

After quite a while, with sand still swirling through the air, and no better vision than we'd had, Irva Lee suddenly exclaimed, "Liz, I think we should be leaving right now!"

The Holy Spirit prompted and I agreed,"Yes, we should be going!"

I inched out onto the road and drove by "feel' for a couple of miles, going very slowly. We finally came out of the dust storm. Right on our tail was this big bus barreling along the road. The bus driver had driven that route so many times, he was driving it blind, literally, with time-worn familiarity. If we had stayed where we were, we would have been smashed to smithereens. We three girls knew our lives had been spared and we had been blessed with divine intervention. We pulled over to pray our thanks.

When I ran out of money after two years at BYU, my friend Doris and I decided we could earn money in Alaska working in a salmon cannery. She needed money for her mission, and I needed it for my studies in Archaeology and Anthropology. A friend referred us to a cannery on the Kenai Peninsula.

The fish went up every other river but the Kenai River that year. Instead of 16 hours a day, six days a week, we had eight hours a day, two days a week. Doris went over to Kodiak Island and earned enough to finance her mission. I had to stay with my camper vehicle which we'd been living in. I earned very little.

Doris flew home later because there was a lot of work on Kodiak Island. I left Alaska, driving alone, watched over and protected several times. On the old dirt Alcan highway, I had a couple of flat tires, even though I had new Golden Bear Polyester 500's. One flat occurred when I was about to leave one of the infrequent gas stations—a great blessing. The other happened just as I was driving into another gas station—another great blessing because gas stations were 50 miles apart or more.

In the Yukon Territory, after long dusty miles, I stopped at a warm springs for a bath. It was already dark but I didn't want to miss the clean feeling. I walked along a long, narrow wooden walkway set in a sulfur swamp on the way to the warm spring. I carried a two-mantle lantern to light my way. The lantern's lights suddenly went out and I could not see my hand in front of my face.

I immediately sunk to my knees in prayer. Then fumbling in my jeans, I found a book of matches and my lantern gave light again. What an immense relief.

After a very long drive, I arrived back in Provo with $1.25 in my pocket. The next day my battery went dead! I phoned my Mom and asked if she would send me a little loan.

When I was in Montezuma Canyon with the Archaeology School the Summer before, Calvin Walker, the father of our site photographer, Jim Walker, had asked me to teach for him. After returning from Alaska, I called and accepted the job offer.

I found a place to live on the west side of Provo, just off Center Street, in a stationary mobile home on a lot near a big produce garden. A woman there was looking for a roommate, the perfect time for me, needing a place right away upon my return from Alaska. This was on Tuesday. I struck up a conversation with a man tending the garden who happened to be the owner. He had so much produce in the garden that I could take all I wanted—even enough for canning purposes. I got to work right away and canned two dozen bottles each of two kinds of vegetables. After all, I'd seen my Mom do this sort of thing many times.

On Saturday morning, I went out to the mailbox and in it there was a tithing envelope, open, and stuffed full of cash. When I looked at the Bishop's name and address on the envelope, I realized the bishop of what was to be my new ward, had an address with the same north coordinate as mine, but a different west coordinate.

I hopped on my bicycle to deliver the small treasure to the bishop's house. When I arrived, they were having a family birthday party for 8-year-old Marc-Ann. Her mother, two brothers, and grandmother were her party guests.

They exclaimed over the envelope and its contents, thanked me, and invited me for cake and ice cream. As I sat next to Marc-Ann's grandmother, she asked, making conversation, what I'd been doing lately. I proudly replied that I'd been bottling tomatoes and green beans.

"Green beans?" she said. "How long did you process them?"

I answered her promptly, "Twenty-eight minutes, like the tomatoes."

Looking apprehensive, she asked, "When do you plan to eat the green beans?"

"Oh, all year long, I suppose," I casually replied.

"They'll kill you!" was her immediate response.

She went on to tell me about deadly botulism, and how one teaspoon could do me in. I had this wonderful picture of Mom at our wood stove in the cabin at the upper farm, and couldn't comprehend this news right away. I asked if I could phone Mom about her green bean production.

They were eager for me to do so. Mom told me she had processed her green beans for 240 minutes. When my new friend Yvonne got on the phone, my mother thanked her profusely for her intervention. They told me they had never in all their lives seen, or heard of, cash left in an envelope in an open mailbox.

Experiences near water have been especially trying. I took a roommate to Deer Creek Reservoir and we motored out in a 16-foot aluminum boat, normally not dangerous if skirting the shorelines. We were fishing and quite suddenly a storm came up when we were on the far side of the lake. It took every ounce of strength to keep the boat headed in the right direction to get us back in without harm or loss.

Mirror Lake in the Uintahs Mountains also provided similar excitement. We were fishing when a storm swept in. Though it was summer, hail pelted us. The shore and our docking point seemed a long ways away. By the time we got to shore where we'd begun, my arms were very tired from controlling the throttle and fighting the force of the wind, rain, and hail.

The longest and most frightening event came about when I took a group of Young Women canoeing and kayaking on Utah Lake. The Summiteers, or fifth-year girls, were capable campers. We were doing the trip around 27-mile-long Utah Lake instead of a long hike. Our Stake's Young Women had backpacked Yosemite's Half Dome, Calf Creek, to the top of Mt. Timpanogos, The Granddaddies, Grand Tetons, Little Death Hollow, Grand Gulch, and ten miles down to Havasupai at the southwest corner of the Grand Canyon over their camping years. We had many backpacking trips and such good times. All told, I took the Young Women on thirty backpack hikes, in addition to the regular week-long summer camp.

We put the canoes and kayaks in at Provo Boat Harbor and made it to Saratoga where we would meet up with our truck carrying tents, equipment, and food. After camping there for the night, we started off down the west side of the lake, which took all day. We determined to cut across the "thumb" on the southwest corner of the lake so that we would meet our truck on West Mountain's shore on time. Ben, our priesthood leader, had thought three days would be enough time to circumnavigate Utah Lake. That proved to be somewhat optimistic, especially as we fought wind and water all the way down the west side, though the sky was bright and sunny.

We were in the middle of the crossing of the "thumb," a relatively short distance to go, when a terrific storm came up. Storms come up often and suddenly, someone had told me, but from a blue sky? With sunshine?

Because Utah Lake is so shallow—only 13 feet deep at most—the wind causes small waves which are no big deal for larger, motorized boats. However, our canoes struggled. The kayak took a wave broadside and went down. Two people clung to my red Coleman canoe. Then the 15-

foot Smokercraft took a two to three foot wave broadside—and it went down as well.

Now five were clinging to the front, back, and sides of my canoe. Ben and one young woman were holding on up front, one girl was holding on in the back, and there was a girl on each of the sides. We brought one of the girls into the canoe because she'd had an issue at Girls Camp, hyperventilating at the campsite. I needed to keep her busy and distracted so I had her bailing water out of the canoe with her shoe.

For four long hours, we were rained on, hailed on, and lashed about by the wind. I'm sure everyone was praying silently. I was asked to pray aloud, which I did, with all the faith and courage I could find in me. I spoke encouraging words also, like yelling to Ben to tell me when he could feel ground, or even mud, under his feet.

I didn't dare get out of the canoe to let one of the other girls in, because I was the only one with the strength and experience to keep the canoe aimed at the waves to avoid having them hit us broadside. I had heard somewhere that Satan controls the water. I wondered if it was true and if he had the power to take a life. I prayed, "If he can take a life, let it be my life. These young girls have only begun to live. Kaylynne, an assistant leader in the front of my canoe, has a husband and son. Ben has a wife and several children. If someone has to die, let it be me."

Then Ben felt mud under his feet. I jumped out to help push the canoe. The girl who had been hanging on the back all that time got into the canoe in my place. Ben and I tugged the canoe toward shore some distance away.

The lake water lifted us up on the waves, then let us sink into the troughs. We were alternating having our heads above the water, then under the water. When we finally reached shore, we pulled the girls out of the canoe and into a tight circle, hugging and praying our thanks for deliverance.

Our truck driver missed us when we didn't arrive on time. He contacted some of our people and was about to call the Utah Lake equivalent of the Coast Guard when he spotted us on the shore. More calls were made and parents notified. Two girls who couldn't make it on our canoe trip because of college entrance tests felt bad because they'd missed the adventure!

One night I woke up at midnight, feeling very sick, almost paralyzed. I could barely get to the phone. I called my friends, Linda and Jon. Jon came and took me to the emergency room at the hospital in Orem. The doctor on call took all my vital signs and said he couldn't find anything wrong with me. He probably thought I was a hypochondriac and he was going to send me home to go to my regular doctor in the morning.

I was afraid to leave because I knew something was very wrong. I said, "I'm not going anywhere until you find something, so you better get at it!"

I have a problem registering an elevated temperature, even when I have an infection so I convinced him to look further. He reluctantly took a blood sample. When the results came back, they whisked me into a bed. I had a staph infection in a lymph node. They would fight for six days to save my life. The day I left the hospital, a nurse said, "If you had come in one day later, you would have gone out horizontal!"

The Blessings of Challenge

I have been blessed to serve two missions from home at the Church Office Building as a hostess, and at the Missionary Training Center in the Reading Office. I've been privileged to do genealogy work. I know I've been guided, guarded, and protected. There are many more miracles of preservation, and blessing, that I haven't included here.

I know that the challenges I have faced, and those I am still facing, are blessings. These experiences, and many others, remind me that it is imperative that we face the storms of life with courage, calling on God to help us in our extremity. "Why me?" need not pass our lips. "Why not me?" would make more sense, as we all go through life's storms at various times.

Challenges get me to go in the direction I need to go. Prayers are answered in the best possible way for us. There are three answers to prayer: "yes," "not now," and "I've got something better planned for you." Each and every one of us is valuable in the eyes of our Father in Heaven.

We all have good and great things to do. As Abraham Lincoln said, "We are all about as happy as we mean to be." This knowledge motivates me to want to do good.

Photo Gallery

The Fourth Grade Team at Orchard Elementary. I taught Utah History and Science.

The Fourth Grade Team at Orchard Elementary—having some fun.

Brain Page, principal at Orchard Elementary
with Miss Sartori's second graders; 1983.

Students displaying Lamp of Knowledge reading trophies earned by reading 1500 pages every two months consistently through the entire year.

Bradly, Kristy, Cameron, Monica and the other students *earned* the privilege of holding Rosie's Golden Retriever puppies by reading 1500 pages in two months time. We forgot two puppies the box! Taken at UVU campus.

Tae Kwon Do Team

We did Tae Kwon Do in P.E. for three years, thanks to my friend, Mary Louise Zeller, a national champion. On school festival day, we did Tai Kwon Do routines to music, like "Eye of the Tiger" and "We Are the Champions."

Four students who went on to earn all of their belts.

One of our field trips to the Dinosaur Museum at Brigham Young University.

Gifted and Talented students from Orchard Elementary. Students were selected from four second grade classrooms and taught my Miss Sartori.

One of many cards received from students. This one is from Nicole Nielsen.

Miss Sartori

Picture Essay

DAR Children's Contest

The booklet on the next several pages was created by second grade students. It was an entry in the DAR (Daughters of the American Revolution) Children's Contest. The theme was "Educators."

The students chose to do the Picture Essay part of the contest. They selected the photos from a huge pile, then asked me about them. They wrote the captions in their own words.

It was a winner! The four students who worked on it received awards and the essay went all the way to nationals.

This is Miss Sartori's favorite quote.

National Society Daughters Of The American Revolution

JUNIOR AMERICAN CITIZENS COMMITTEE

This is to certify that Elizabeth Ann Sartori

Has been awarded The Thatcher Award

By Utah State DAR

For Outstanding Patriotism 1993-1994

National Theme Flags in American History

Signed Alice L. Astroth

Title State Regent

Date April 1994

Miss Sartori won several medals and awards.
She is in Who's Who Among America's Teachers.
Here she is getting an award for patriotism
from the D.A.R.

She was once a little girl like me.
She is the one on the right.

Ms. Sartori was graduated from B.Y.U.
with Masters Degree in Education in a cap and gown.

She likes to go on trips with her friends.
Here she is in Cancun.

She likes sewing.
She sewed these dresses.

She likes
to go
hiking

and backpacking

and
camping.

She liked to study archaeology
and she likes to go bike-riding.

Her friends took her out to dinner on her birthday.
She likes to go out to dinner with her friends.

Miss Sartori – some former students.
Some times she gets invited to their weddings and their homes.

She also went to Butch Cassidy's Robbers' Roost.
And she went to where Butch had his horses drink water.
She went with a family of her student's.

Miss Sartori has had some people come to her class and talk about things they do.

She sometimes gives her tutor students rewards. She once took a student to the zoo to ride an elephant at the end of the summer.

Miss Sartori likes to see kids get medals and trophies and this kid got a running trophy.

Kids who read 8,000 pages of Recreational Reading by the end of the year got their pic. taken for the newspaper and got a trophy of the Lamp of Knowledge.

Miss Sartori let her students do something called the "Invent America" Social Studies project.

Amy's Mom wanted to take a picture of Miss Sartori and Amy together.

Miss Sartori took the kids on a field trip to B.Y.U. at the Monte L. Bean Museum and the Reptile Labs.

She let one of her students stand beside a dinosaur's leg bone. On another trip she let her students see her in a fireman's suit.

She shares her toys with her friends!

Miss Sartori also used to let her class
hold the pet boa constrictor, "Crictor".

She likes her students and her students like her.

When her class studied Japan, they had Girls' Day and Boys' Day to celebrate Japanese holidays. The girls brought their dolls.

Sometimes students have run 100 miles during the school year, and different years she does Tae Kwon Do. Sometimes she gives some trophies if they run two hundred miles.

This is one of her favorite quotes.

Last, but not least, another favorite quote—that's what Miss Sartori said.

Retirement Party

What a party the faculty threw for me! The wrapped gift is a beautiful print of a green canyon with an eagle flying overhead. Perfect!

Three of the kids from the Edwin Spann family.
I had five children from that family come through my classes.

I got to be a real show-off with my quilts, journals and other projects.

Linda Horsely Cook, my friend of 38 years, is giving me a hug at my retirement party.

A stitchery done by Amy Blake Spencer for Miss Sartori, her elementary teacher.

Julie Christensen, former kindergartner, stitched this for me when she was in high school at Orem High.

I taught at Orchard Elementary
for fifteen years. We had an
extended year program,
initiated by principal,
Brian Page.
Parents could choose
track or teacher.

Here are three of the
Carter children and
their wedding invitations–

Sydney and her
sweetheart, Owen
(left)

Ned and his
sweetheart, Nicole
(right)

Hannah and her sweetheart, Brad

Brekke Fernlund and her sweetheart, Bill. I was her teacher in second grade. When they moved into my ward, she became *my* teacher—my visiting teacher!

Matthew Melville
and his sweetheart,
Lecia Marie

K.J. Stratton
and his
sweetheart

Here are two children from the Vineyard family. Four of the Vineyard children came through my classes.

Michael and his sweetheart, Catherine

Christy Marie and her sweetheart

Four children from the Alan and Edel Lambson family came through my classes. They are now all grown.

The mother of this family, Pamela Ellis Dahl, was once my kindergartner.

Through the Years

Top left: From, a mission plaque and in a book of genealogy.
Top right: In the Alps, on a trip to Europe.
Middle right: Thanksgiving weekend, selecting Christmas trees in the National Forest; guest of Linda Spencer's family.
Bottom center: Receiving the Thatcher Award from the DAR.

Christmas Party

The "one true shift" enjoys lots of fun, good friends, and great food!

Pictures from
the Christmas Party
we held for the
hostesses at the
Church Office Building,
during my mission
from home.

2007 Trip to Israel

During my trip to Israel in 1997.
I'd always wanted to ride a camel!

On top of Masada in Israel

Swimming in the Dead Sea

2007 Trip to Australia

Hugging a koala!

On the way out to the Great Barrier Reef to go snorkeling

In the bay on the Gold Coast

2008 Trip to Peru

Lake Titicaca in the Peruvian Highlands

I make friends wherever I go!

Machu Pichu, Peru

The Stanton Family

Dear friend, Virginia Stanton, marrying Jim Woods in the Manti Temple. (top left)

The Stanton Clan—all these children are now grown. (middle)

Evelyn Nelson Stanton—my "mom" in the church from Park City, Utah

About the Author

Liz Sartori taught elementary school for thirty-five years—three in Connecticut, and thirty-two years in Utah. She supervised student teachers one year for Brigham Young University's Education Department in the middle of her teaching career. She is in Who's Who Among America's Teachers. Liz feels her greatest rewards are the children who have come back to visit her as adults, who have shared favorite memories, invited her to mission farewells and weddings, and who attended her retirement celebration.

As an educator, youth and family camp counselor, and scout leader of Cub Scouts, Webelos, Boy Scouts, and Special Interest Boy Scouts Search and Rescue, Liz truly appreciates getting to know and serve people who have blessed her life so abundantly. Liz acknowledges her work with the Disaster Action Team of the Red Cross (DAT), and her CERT (Community Emergency Response Team) training, for opportunities to learn and serve.

Liz received her Bachelors Degree from Central Connecticut State College in New Britain, Connecticut, and her Masters Degree from Brigham Young University. She has two years toward a Masters Degree in Archaeology and Anthropology from BYU and maintains a life-long interest in those subjects. Liz was also presented with the Thatcher Award for Patriotism from the Daughters of the American Revolution (DAR).

Made in the USA
Monee, IL
13 August 2020

37411928R00075